Clueless in the Kitchen

BY EVELYN RAAB

There's everything to eat here

FIREFLY BOOKS

A Firefly Book

Published by Firefly Books Ltd. 2011

First printing

Publisher Cataloging-in-Publication Data (U.S.)

Raab, Evelyn.
     Clueless in the kitchen : a cookbook for teens / Evelyn Raab ;
illustrated by George A. Walker.
Includes index.
Summary: Recipes and meal preparation tips for inexperienced teens.
ISBN-13: 978-1-55407-824-0 (pbk.)
1. Cooking — Juvenile literature. 2. Cookery. I. Walker, George A. II. Title.
641.5 dc22   TX652.5R333   2011

Library and Archives Canada Cataloguing in Publication

Raab, Evelyn
     Clueless in the kitchen : a cookbook for teens / Evelyn Raab.
Includes index.
ISBN-13: 978-1-55407-824-0
     1. Cooking — J uvenile literature. 2. Cookbooks. I. Title.
TX652.5.R32 2011   j641.5'123   C2011-902320-2

Published in the United States by
Firefly Books (U.S.) Inc.
P.O. Box 1338, Ellicott Station
Buffalo, New York 14205

Published in Canada by
Firefly Books Ltd.
66 Leek Crescent
Richmond Hill, Ontario L4B 1H1

Illustrations: George A. Walker
Design: Jean Lightfoot Peters

Printed in Canada

The publisher gratefully acknowledges the financial support for our publishing program by the Government of Canada through the Canada Book Fund as administered by the Department of Canadian Heritage.

Contents

Starting from Scratch

How you ended up with this book is not important. Maybe your parents gave it to you. Maybe you bought it for yourself. Maybe you found it in a ditch. It doesn't matter. The thing is, you have it, and now you have to use it. But how?

So this is a cookbook. You've probably already noticed that. And it's full of recipes—which is pretty much what you'd expect. These recipes are simple without being stupid. They contain no scary terminology, no really strange ingredients, no complicated procedures. They also contain (almost) no processed foods—no cake mixes, no condensed tomato soups, no frozen whipped toppings. You don't need them. Ever. Cooking from scratch is easy and cheap, and *always* tastes better. That's a fact.

This book is full of other stuff you need to know too. Kitchen stuff. Basic stuff that no one ever bothered to tell you. Or maybe you weren't listening. And now you're sorry, because *now* you want to know. *Now* the kitchen needs sanitizing, or *now* you have to cut up a chicken or have to (*yikes!*) convert measurements. And you *certainly* don't want

to go crawling back to Mom, do you? You'll also find information on how to shop, where to find specialty items and how to plan a meal.

So how do you get started? Well, just start. Find something you want to cook and cook it. Go ahead—be brave. After all, cooking isn't brain surgery. It just *looks* like it.

Key to Recipe Types

The following icons identify the various types of recipes in this book. A recipe may have several icons, suggesting that it falls into many categories.

Cheap Eats

Oh, stop feeling so sorry for yourself. We're all broke sometimes. Eating cheaply doesn't mean eating bad food. It doesn't have to mean surviving on a dreary menu of canned beans and baloney, boxed macaroni-and-cheese dinners and day-old doughnuts. Unless, of course, you want it to. But that's your business.

Learn to cook and you'll always eat well without spending a fortune. Some of the best things in life are cheap.

Mom Food

Who fed you chicken soup when you had a cold? Who waited for you after school with homemade cookies? Who made the best potato salad on the block? Okay, so maybe your mom wasn't much of a cook. And maybe she was too busy driving a backhoe to be around after school. Maybe you never even had a bowl of homemade chicken soup in your life. Well, it's never too late for Mom Food. Even if you have to make it yourself.

Vegetarian

Being a vegetarian doesn't just mean picking all the pepperoni off your take-out pizza or ordering your fries without gravy. No, really, you are going to have to learn to cook a few things if you want your parents to stop freaking out. These recipes contain no meat, poultry or fish, but may contain eggs and dairy.

Cooking to Impress

Most of the time, cooking is a pretty practical business. You cook because you're hungry and you want something to eat. You might make a pot of chili or a casserole or some other normal regular food.

But then there are other times. Birthdays. Anniversaries. Groundhog Day. Or maybe you have an ulterior motive. Maybe you figure a romantic evening over a fondue pot will do the trick. Well, maybe it will.

 Dinner for the Family

Drat. It's 5 p.m. and no one is home. There is no stew bubbling on the stove, no casserole baking in the oven, no apple pie cooling on the counter. There is, however, a package of hamburger in the fridge, a bag of macaroni in the pantry and a note on the table that says, "I'll be home at 7. Make dinner. Love, Mom." So what's a kid supposed to do?

Cook, I guess.

Other Nitpicky Details You May Want to Know

If you have specific dietary issues, you will need to know which recipes are safe for you. These letters will help you identify them:

GF—Gluten-free

EF—Egg-free

DF—Dairy-free

Recipe Abbreviation Decoder

Recipes tend to use a lot of abbreviations. This is not a problem if you've been cooking for a while and know what they mean. But what if you don't? You'll need to know the difference between tsp and tbsp if you want those cookies to turn out perfectly. Here's some help.

tsp—teaspoon

tbsp—tablespoon

lb—pound

oz—ounce (usually used for weight measurement)

qt—quart

pt—pint

fl oz—fluid ounce (usually used for volume measurement)

gal—gallon

ml—milliliter

g—gram

kg—kilogram

cm—centimeter

l—liter

F—Fahrenheit

C—celsius

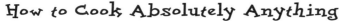

How to Cook Absolutely Anything

Read the recipe. Twice. The first time—to decide if the dish actually sounds like something you want to cook. Or eat. Does the recipe include an ingredient you hate? Does it require a piece of equipment you don't have? Does it take too long to cook? The second time—to read the recipe more c-a-r-e-f-u-l-l-y. Do you have all the ingredients? Are you sure? Didn't your brother eat all the chocolate chips last week? Go check. Now.

Assemble everything you need before you start. Everything. The bowls, the pots, the measuring cups, all the ingredients. Take nothing for granted. You don't want to discover at a critical moment that the 9-inch baking dish you need is in the freezer, half filled with last week's leftover lasagna.

Follow the recipe exactly. This is no time to be rebellious. At least, not the first time. Make the dish once exactly the way the recipe tells you to. Just once. The next time, go ahead and be reckless. Leave out the tomatoes! Double the walnuts! Heck—add some peanut butter! It's your recipe now, baby.

Get over disasters. Everyone has them. Just don't let yourself wallow in them. Pick yourself up, scrape the burned crud off the bottom of the oven, mop up the mess on the floor, feed the disintegrated glop to the dog. And get on with life. It happens.

Know what you like. You can't cook if you don't know what you like to eat. And eating, after all, is the goal. At least, it's supposed be. Know what you enjoy eating and cook what you want to eat, and you'll probably have fun cooking.

Finally—there are no rules. No one owns a recipe, and there is no right or wrong way for something to taste. If you like it, then it's good. If you don't like it, then it's not good. That's all there is to it. Trust yourself.

The Kitchen—A Guide to Alien Territory

Totally Essential Kitchen Stuff

You really need these:

- large frying pan (10 inches/25 cm diameter) or larger
- small frying pan (6 inches/15 cm diameter) or thereabouts
- large pot (6 quarts/liters) or larger *with* a lid
- small saucepan (2½ quarts/liters)
- strainer or colander
- at least 2 mixing bowls—one large and one small (and more is better)
- microwave-safe casserole (2 to 3 quarts/liters) with a lid
- small sharp paring knife
- large sharp knife
- wooden cutting board
- wooden spoon for cooking
- cookie sheet (2 if possible)
- muffin pan (12-cup)
- measuring cup
- set of measuring spoons
- grater
- pot holders or oven mitts
- can opener

Very Nice to Have, but Not Essential

- a really big stock pot for making a huge vat of soup or spaghetti sauce
- collapsible vegetable steamer
- kitchen scissors
- roasting pan
- loaf pan
- pie pan
- soup ladle
- metal tongs
- vegetable peeler
- wire whisk
- blender
- electric mixer
- microwave oven
- food processor
- toaster
- rubber or silicone scraper
- metal spatula (lifter)
- wok
- garlic press
- potato masher

Storing Food—What Should Go Where

You bought it—now, where do you keep it? Rule of thumb: when in doubt, keep it in the fridge. Except, of course, if it's frozen.

In the cupboard or pantry

- flour and sugar
- pasta, rice, grains, beans
- canned foods
- unopened jars of jam, mayonnaise, ketchup, pickles, salad dressing, stuff like that
- vinegar
- chocolate
- spices and dried herbs
- onions and garlic
- potatoes
- soup mixes
- cookies, cake
- nuts (or refrigerate for extended storage)
- vegetable oil or olive oil

In the fridge

- eggs
- cheese
- other dairy products
- most fresh vegetables and fruit
- meat, fish, poultry
- open jars of jam, mayonnaise, ketchup, pickles, salad dressing, stuff like that
- cooked leftovers
- bread (for longer storage)

In the freezer

- baked things—bread, cakes, cookies (anything you won't be using soon)
- frozen foods, obviously
- ice cream

Basic Kitchen Sanitation—a Matter of Life and Death

You *definitely* don't want food poisoning. Besides being totally disgusting, it could actually kill you, which is not a good thing. So how do you avoid this experience? The following food-handling safety tips might help:

Don't thaw frozen foods on the kitchen counter. Bacteria grow quickly at room temperature, rapidly turning your ground beef into a toxic time bomb. Thaw frozen meat overnight in the refrigerator or defrost in the microwave just before cooking.

When in doubt, throw it out! If meat or other food looks or smells weird, cooking will not make it safe to eat. Just get rid of it and order a pizza instead.

Keep your work areas clean. This isn't just a mom thing—it's an actual safety thing. Wash your hands, cutting board and utensils in hot soapy water before and after messing around with food. Cross-contamination is a real danger. It happens when bacteria-laden juices from raw meat or poultry contact a surface (your cutting board, knife or hands) that then contaminates another food (such as bread or lettuce). Keep cooked and raw foods entirely separate, and wash or sanitize all cooking utensils and surfaces after using. Better to be crazy clean than sick.

Forget the rare hamburger. Just forget it. Ground meats—beef, chicken, pork, turkey—are especially dangerous, because when meat is ground, the outer surface (which may be teeming with bacteria) is mixed throughout the meat. Cook any type of ground meat until you can no longer see any pink, and don't even think about eating any of that stuff raw.

Don't let cooked foods hang around at room temperature. Keep cold foods cold and hot foods hot. That leftover lasagna? Stick it right into the fridge—don't leave it loitering on the counter.

Watch that potato salad! Keep all salads made with eggs or mayonnaise refrigerated until serving time. Going on a picnic? Use a vinaigrette as a dressing instead of mayo—you'll find a basic vinaigrette recipe in this book. How embarrassing if you poisoned Aunt Mildred.

Shopping

Kitchen Staples

You're hungry. You're in the mood to cook something. You're not in the mood to go shopping. If you keep a few basic groceries on hand, you'll always be able to whip something up.

- flour
- sugar
- coffee and tea
- salt and pepper
- rice
- vegetable or olive oil
- oatmeal
- chocolate chips
- canned beans
- bouillon cubes or powder
- pasta and spaghetti sauce
- canned tomatoes
- canned tuna
- baking powder
- baking soda
- eggs
- milk
- onions
- carrots
- potatoes
- garlic
- bread
- peanut butter
- jam
- cheese
- apples
- butter or margarine
- cinnamon

Supermarket Strategies

Supermarkets are in the business of selling as much stuff as they possibly can. And they do it very well. When you go shopping, be aware of the booby traps that await an unsuspecting consumer— and avoid them.

Big rule: never shop hungry. Eat something *(anything)* before you step a single toe inside the supermarket, or else you'll find yourself buying things you would normally be able to resist. If you don't think this is true, just try to walk down the bakery aisle without buying anything when you haven't eaten lunch.

Buy store-label brands. These are usually cheaper than name-brand products and often just as good. In fact, you might even like the store-brand potato chips or cookies better than your usual kind.

Buy big only when it makes sense. If you can't use up that humongous jar of jam before it goes bad, then it doesn't make sense to buy it. On the other hand, if a five-pound bag of carrots costs just a few pennies more than a two-pound bag, go for it—just don't forget to eat the carrots.

Beware the ends of the aisles. Don't assume that just because something is displayed at the end of an aisle it's on sale. Sometimes it's not. Very sneaky. Check the price.

Buy only what you really need. Make a list at home and take it with you to the store. If you just need milk and a loaf of bread, go straight for those items, pay for them and leave the store. Immediately. Do not walk past the cookies. Do not linger at the ice cream.

Don't buy three peppers if you only want one. If the store has wrapped fresh vegetables into packages of two or more, ask the produce person (nicely) to (please) remove one pepper and price it for you. They *will* do that.

Check the dates on perishable items. Dairy products like milk and yogurt, baked goods like bread and rolls, and many other perishable foods are stamped with a Best Before date. This just means what it says: the item is best before a certain date. It does *not* mean that the item is automatically rotten the day after that date—but it might be. Always look for the item with the longest expiry date to get the freshest stock.

Don't even glance at the junk around the checkout counter. This is where they put all the stuff no one needs. They are counting on you to surrender to impulse and buy a chocolate bar or a magazine or a package of gum. You are being manipulated! You must resist!

How to Buy Fruits and Vegetables

It's a jungle out there! Step into the produce section of any supermarket and you're instantly overwhelmed. There are oranges and apples and grapes and bananas. There are onions and eggplants and tomatoes and seven kinds of lettuce. There are fruits you've never seen before and stuff you don't know what to do with. So? What are you waiting for—an engraved invitation? Go buy something. Here are some words of wisdom to help you navigate this confusing area.

Fresh fruits and vegetables should look and smell fresh. They should be firm and shiny, with no rotten spots. This doesn't mean you can't use an apple with a bruise on it, or a slightly droopy string bean. But if you're paying top dollar for fresh produce, inspect it carefully to make sure it really is worth buying. If it isn't, don't buy it.

Whenever possible, buy what's in season. It will likely be inexpensive and better quality than out-of-season produce. Eat apples in the fall, oranges in the winter, asparagus in the spring and peaches in the summer.

Buy locally grown fruits and vegetables whenever possible. Why would anyone buy imported tomatoes in August when the local ones are delicious and abundant? This, of course, does not apply to things such as bananas unless you happen to live in Costa Rica. Ask questions and shop smart.

Shop at farmers' markets whenever you can. Getting involved with your cauliflower is easy when you've talked to the guy who grew it. And there's no better way to make sure the stuff is really fresh. Plus, it's a great way to learn about local food. You might even get some ideas on how to cook what you've bought.

Don't buy more than you can possibly use. Buying a huge basket of fresh peaches is pointless if you can't eat them all before they rot.

Check out the clearance bin! Sometimes you can find wonderful bargains. Lots of marked-down produce is perfect if you plan to eat it or cook with it right away. The bin is a haven for banana bread bakers and soup lovers.

Buy Brussels sprouts even if you think you hate them. Just once. Maybe you hate them because of how your grandma cooked them. Maybe you'll *love* them the way you cook them. You'll never know unless you try. This also goes for squash.

Who cares what it is—just try it! No vegetable will kill you, even if you eat one raw that should have been cooked, or cooked one better left raw. Even a potato eaten raw isn't toxic—although it may be unusual. So don't be afraid of buying something unfamiliar just because you don't know what to do with it. Think of it as an opportunity to do some potentially delicious research and experimentation.

How to Buy Meat

Meat is scary. It comes with no cooking instructions, it all looks identical and the same chunk of meat may have several different names. That's almost enough to turn a person into a vegetarian. Or not.

Make friends with a butcher. Ask stupid questions: What is this? What do you do with it? Is it any good? Most butchers are only too happy to share pearls of carnivorous wisdom with anyone who is interested. An especially enthusiastic butcher may even divulge a favorite recipe.

The hamburger dilemma. Ground chuck? Ground sirloin? Ground round? Twenty percent fat? Fifteen percent fat? Thirty percent fat? Such a basic food item—how do you decide what to buy? Generally, the higher the percentage of fat, the less expensive the meat; the leaner the meat, the more expensive it will be. Buy lean or extra-lean ground beef (10 percent fat or less) when you're making something like hamburgers or meat loaf—where the fat doesn't really get a chance to drain off. You can get away with a cheaper, regular ground beef (up to 30 percent fat) if you're making chili or spaghetti sauce—where you can drain away the excess fat after browning. A good compromise for most purposes is medium ground beef with 15 to 20 percent fat. Many supermarkets mark their ground beef with these percentages to help you choose; others will simply label ground beef as regular, medium, lean or extra lean.

What about ground turkey, chicken, lamb and pork? Go ahead and try them instead of ground beef in your favorite recipe. The taste and texture will be different, but your substitution will work—you may even like your variation better.

No, sausages are not made from ground-up rats. Meat regulations are extremely strict, so unless you buy sausages from some guy named Igor down the street who makes them in his basement, you can be pretty sure you're safe as long as the meat has been properly handled and cooked.

Roasts can be intimidating. Most big hunks of meat look alike, more or less. But they aren't alike. Ask anyone who has ever tried to roast a tough hunk of stewing beef. If you don't know what you want to

make, buy meat that's on sale and ask the butcher (or your mom) how to cook it. If you have a specific dish in mind, find out which cut of meat is appropriate. Either way, you'll have to do some homework.

Not all steaks are created equal. Only a select few types of steak are tender enough to slap on the barbecue just the way they are. Others need to be marinated before cooking. Still others should be gently simmered in some stewy concoction.

Rule of thumb: Meat from the back end of the animal is more tender than meat from the front. Learn your animal anatomy by consulting a meat chart or asking the butcher.

A Brief Compendium of Meat
or
Help! How Do You Cook This Thing?

Fire up the barbecue	Tender and roast-worthy	Slow and steady—stew, pot-roast or braise with liquid
beef rib and rib-eye steak	beef rib roast	beef chuck, blade or shoulder
beef strip loin or New York steak	beef sirloin roast	beef bottom round
beef tenderloin or filet mignon	beef top round or eye-of-round roast	beef brisket
beef sirloin	beef tenderloin	beef short ribs
beef flank steak	pork loin	beef stewing meat
any ground meat	pork leg or ham	pork shoulder roast or chops
sausages and hot dogs	lamb leg or shoulder	lamb shoulder or stewing lamb
lamb chops	chicken	chicken
pork rib or loin chops	turkey	turkey thighs
pork tenderloin	duck	
pork spare ribs		
ham steak		
chicken, whole or parts		
turkey breast cutlets		

Cheese Shopping—an Adventure

There are (approximately) seventeen zillion kinds of cheese in the world. So why do you always buy that flat, plastic-wrapped kind? Why not take a chance and try a tiny sliver of something new? Hey, you might even fall in love!

A cheese store is a wonderful place. It's stinky, filled with weird, wonderful things and often run by someone who really knows and loves cheese. Best of all, a cheese store—a good one—will let you taste before you buy—which is nice when you really don't know what you're looking for. It's even nice when you *do* know. Don't be afraid to sound like an idiot—tell the cheese person you're new to cheese shopping and you want to try something different. Try a really stinky cheese, or a blue cheese or a sharp cheese. If you're timid, ask for something mild and then work your way up. How will you ever know what you like unless you experiment? Go ahead—be daring.

The following extremely incomplete list will give you a start on your cheese adventures. After that, you're on your own.

For slicing and in sandwiches
Havarti, Monterey Jack, Muenster, brick, cheddar, Colby, Edam, Emmentaler, Swiss, Jarlsberg, fontina, Gouda, provolone, Asiago

For cooking, melting and casseroles
Mozzarella, Monterey Jack, cheddar, Colby, Emmentaler, Swiss, Jarlsberg, fontina, Parmesan, Romano, Gruyère

On crackers for a snack or appetizer
Brie, Camembert, Havarti, Muenster, Saint Paulin, cheddar, Colby, Stilton blue, Edam, Emmentaler, Swiss, Jarlsberg, Gouda, goat cheese

In salads
Feta, cheddar, Parmesan, Danish blue, Roquefort, bocconcini

The Freezer Zone

What lurks behind the glass doors of your supermarket's freezer section? Well, almost everything, really.

The frozen food section of a supermarket is a minefield. If you're not careful, you can end up with lots of overpriced, overprocessed junk.

But if you are careful, you can find plenty of stuff that's inexpensive, nutritious and convenient. Tread carefully and you'll be fine.

Buy frozen foods that are as close to their original state as possible. This means that frozen fish fillets are a good choice, but frozen, breaded fish fillets with marinara sauce and pizza cheese may not be. Plain frozen peas are great, but boil-in-the-bag peas with French onion gravy are not. The less processing a frozen food has endured, the less junk will have been added to it and the cheaper (and better) it will be.

Stay away—far away—from frozen dinners. Sure, the trays are cute and in ten minutes you've got a total meal. With dessert, even. But it's not worth it. The food is almost always overprocessed, overcooked and overpriced. In a big hurry? You're better off to scramble an egg, cut up some fresh veggies and toast a bagel. Need dessert? Have an apple.

What about frozen pizza? Well, it's cheaper than ordering in and sometimes it's decent enough. So, okay, keep one in the freezer for an emergency. As a main dish when it's been one of those days, a pizza beats a bag of potato chips—just don't make a regular habit of it. Other items that might be handy to keep in your freezer: prepared meat, chicken pies or lasagna.

Alternative Shopping

The supermarket isn't the only place to get food. It isn't even a particularly interesting place to get food. Branch out a little. Explore an Asian grocery. Investigate your local farmers' market. Be bold—buy something you don't recognize from a street vendor. Shop on the edge.

International grocery stores

There are Asian grocery stores, Middle Eastern grocery stores and Indian grocery stores. There are shops that sell Latin American foods and shops that sell Italian foods. Every city has a few shops (sometimes entire neighborhoods) that carry products used in the cooking of a particular country or region. The shopkeepers are often delighted to share their culinary secrets—you may come away with a bagful of strange groceries and a few interesting recipes to go with them. Or use the internet as a resource to hunt down recipes for your favorite ethnic dishes and then go shopping for the ingredients. Either way you're guaranteed a delicious adventure.

17

Farmers' markets

Farmers' markets can supply you with four kinds of potatoes, six kinds of beans, three kinds of cucumbers—did you even know they existed? Eggs that are white, brown or blue, locally produced honey and ultrahot horseradish. How can you resist buying a basket of peaches from the person who picked them? Talk to the pie lady or the organic chicken people or the cheese guys and you may just learn a little something. Get up early, hike out to your local farmers' market and check out what's growing these days.

Junk Food—or Is It?

What is junk food, anyway? Is pizza bad or good? Are French fries junk? And what about gummy worms? How's a person to know?

Junk food is any food that doesn't contain enough nutrients to make it worth its weight in calories. Some junk food doesn't contain *any* nutrients. Any food high in sugar or fat, with very little redeeming protein, vitamins or fiber—gummy worms, sorry—is probably junk. On the other hand, pizza—which *can* be pretty salty and high in fat—is still okay (in moderation) because it also happens to be loaded with vegetables, cheese and other good stuff like that.

Occasionally a food gets a bad reputation just because it hangs around with the wrong crowd. Popcorn, for instance. Drench it in butter and salt and it's junk. Even microwave popcorn is often overly salty and too high in fat. But get it on its own or with a sprinkle of cheese and a little salt, and it's a different snack altogether, high in fiber and low in calories. And it still tastes good. Actually, better.

Then there are the junk foods *pretending* to be good for you—like granola bars, and chewy fruit snacks. Many commercial granola bars are too high in sugar and fat to be *really* nutritious snacks. And the ones covered with chocolate are, let's face it, chocolate bars. Fruit snacks are candy. Period. If you want a treat, have one of these. If you want fruit—have a real piece of fruit.

How should you make your choices?

First, read the ingredients. Is sugar heading the list? Junk. If you really want some junk, have it and get it over with. Then eat good stuff for the rest of the day. You don't have to give up eating chocolate bars and cheese puffs completely in order to have a healthy diet. Just don't let junk food *be* your diet. After all, you are what you eat. A scary thought, isn't it?

Your Friend the Bulk Food Store

So you buy a jar of oregano. The oregano weighs half an ounce. The jar (the jar!) weighs over four ounces. Does this make sense? What are you buying, anyhow—the jar or what's inside it? The dried herbs and spices sold in supermarkets are notoriously overpackaged. Buy herbs and spices from a bulk food store and keep them in airtight recycled jars, and you'll save money while you cut down on garbage.

Buy exactly the amount you need. Don't buy a one-pound bag of walnuts when you really only need a few. On the other hand, if you really go through the chocolate chips (and who doesn't?), keep a big jar filled with them to avoid those emergency midnight trips to the corner convenience store.

Buying in bulk is cheaper. You'll save about 30 percent over the supermarket price on most items when you shop at a bulk food store. Pretty amazing when you think about it.

Bring your own bags when you go shopping and whenever possible, refill your old containers. Hooray for less waste!

Those Scary Herbs and Spices

They *are* scary. There are too many of them, and you never have the one you need. The mere mention of *coriander* causes your hands to shake (see, it's happening already). Never mind *cardamom*. Help!

Okay, calm down. Deep dark secret time: there isn't a single recipe that won't work anyway if you leave out every single herb and spice. Not that you *should*, but you *can*. The food won't taste the same, but it will still be edible. You can also put in more or less of an herb than the recipe calls for and, even more shocking, you can substitute an entirely different herb or spice altogether if you want to.

So do something wild. Use cumin instead of caraway! Substitute oregano for basil! Leave out the cinnamon! Double the curry powder!

Look at you go! And you didn't think you were the reckless type.

Bare Bones Spice Collection

What can't you do without?
salt and pepper

What else?
basil
oregano
cinnamon
paprika
fresh garlic
fresh parsley

Want to add just a few more?
cayenne pepper
curry powder
ginger
cumin
thyme
vanilla
Mexican chili powder

Breakfast

 ## Oatmeal from Scratch EF DF

You don't have to buy expensive packets of instant oatmeal in order to have it for breakfast. Quick-cooking natural oats are rolled thin so they cook fast. Old-fashioned rolled oats take a bit longer to cook, but are a hearty alternative. Try both and see which you like.

Stovetop method

| 1 cup (250 ml) | cold water |
| ½ cup (125 ml) | quick-cooking rolled oats (not instant) |

In a small saucepan, combine the water and the oats and bring to a boil over medium heat. Cook, stirring, for about 5 minutes, or until as thick as you like it.

Serve drizzled with honey, sprinkled with brown sugar and cinnamon, swimming in maple syrup, glopped with strawberry jam or drowned in milk.

That's it. Done.

One gooey, warm serving.

Microwave method

| 1 cup (250 ml) | cold water |
| ½ cup (125 ml) | quick-cooking rolled oats (not instant) |

In a large microwave-safe bowl, mix the water and oats. Microwave on high power for 2 minutes, stir, then microwave for another 1 or 2 minutes, stirring every 30 seconds until thickened to your taste.

Can you believe this?

One serving.

How to Boil Water

Fill pot with water.
Put on stove.
Turn heat on high.
Bring to a boil. Serve.

How to Boil an Egg

You feel cruddy. You want an egg. With some toast. Cut into triangles. Just like when you were little. Go ahead, it'll make you feel better.

To make a boiled egg, take your egg and put it in a small saucepan with enough cold water to cover it completely. Bring the water to a boil over medium heat. As soon as the water reaches the boiling point, cover the pan with the lid and *turn off the heat*. Start timing your egg from this point:

20

Runny egg—1 minute
Soft egg—2 minutes
Soft egg with no gooey spots—4 minutes
Hard-cooked egg—15 minutes

This method is guaranteed to give you a *perfectly* cooked egg that will not have exploded in the water. Place it in a nice "eggy" cup, sprinkle with a little salt and pepper and eat it with your favorite Donald Duck spoon while you watch cartoons in your pajamas.

Basic Scrambled Eggs GF DF

Some people scramble eggs slowly over low heat; others flash-scramble them over high heat until the eggs are nearly petrified. Some people add milk; others don't. Feel free to develop your own personal scrambling style from this basic recipe.

Frying-pan method

2	eggs
1 tbsp (15 ml)	milk
2 tsp (10 ml)	butter

Crack the eggs into a small bowl, add the milk and beat with a fork just until the yolks and whites are combined.

Melt the butter in a small frying pan over medium heat and cook until it gets foamy. When the foam subsides, pour in the eggs. Stir constantly with a fork or a wooden spoon until the eggs are almost set and scrambled the way you like them. Eggs will continue to cook for a minute or two after your remove the pan from the heat, so it's better to undercook them slightly.

Makes 1 serving.

Microwave method

2	eggs
1 tbsp (15 ml)	milk
2 tsp (10 ml)	butter

Measure the butter into a small microwave-safe dish and microwave it on high power for 30 to 45 seconds, until melted and hot.

Meanwhile, beat together the eggs and the milk until well combined. Add to the melted butter in the dish. Cook on high power, stirring every 30 seconds, for 1 to 1½ minutes.

Makes 1 serving. (For 2 servings, double the ingredients and cook on high power for 2½ to 3 minutes, stirring every 30 seconds.)

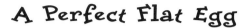

A Perfect Flat Egg

Cooking a fried egg isn't rocket science, but it does take a little finesse. So pay attention.

To cook one perfect flat egg

Melt 1 tbsp (15 ml) butter in a small frying pan over medium heat. Let it get foamy, and when the foam subsides, adjust the heat to low and *very carefully* crack in the egg. *Do not* attempt to drop the egg from a great height into the pan, because the yolk will break and you will no longer have a *perfect* egg. The egg will bubble and splatter a little, but if it's going berserk in the pan, you have the heat up too high, so turn it down a notch.

Let your egg continue to cook over low heat until you begin to see bubbles rising from the bottom of the yolk. Gently lift the edge of the white to find out if it's starting to brown on the bottom. If you like your egg sunny-side up, then it's probably done. If the top is still too runny, cover the pan with a lid for just a minute so the egg sets, then lift carefully from the pan and serve.

If you are an easy-over person, *very, very, gently* lift the egg with a pancake turner and *carefully* flip it onto the other side. The big trick again is to avoid breaking the yolk. Let the egg cook for no more than 30 seconds. You may need a bit of practice until you get it right—but you will.

Done. Perfect.

Next time try cooking two at once!

How to Cook Bacon

In a skillet

Lay as many slices into a *cold* skillet as will fit without overlapping them. (Well, they shouldn't overlap *too much*, anyway.) Adjust the burner to medium heat and cook for 6 to 8 minutes, flipping and rearranging the slices often, until they're done the way you like—crisp or still a bit floppy. Drain slices on a paper towel-lined plate for a minute before serving.

In the microwave

On a microwave roasting rack (if you have one) or in a microwave-safe baking dish, arrange up to 8 slices of bacon in 1 layer. *Don't* overlap them here. Cover with a single layer of paper towel. Microwave on

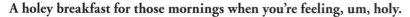

high power for 45 seconds to 1 minute per strip of bacon. Halfway through the cooking time, turn the strips over and rearrange them so that they cook evenly.

Egg-in-the-Hole

A holey breakfast for those mornings when you're feeling, um, holy.

1 tbsp (15 ml)	butter (approximately)
1 slice	white or whole wheat sandwich bread
1	egg

Butter the slice of bread generously on one side. Using a 2½-inch (6 cm) round cookie cutter or an overturned glass of about the same diameter, cut a hole in the middle of the slice of bread. Eat the middle immediately or save it for later. Whatever.

Lay the holey bread slice in a small frying pan, buttered-side down, and place pan over medium heat. Cook until the bread is just lightly toasted on the bottom. Remove it from the pan with a spatula. Add 2 tsp (10 ml) of butter to the pan and spread it around to cover the bottom as it melts. Return the bread to the pan, *toasted-side up.* Immediately crack an egg into the hole. It should just fit without too much leakage out the sides or top. Try not to break the yolk.

Reduce the heat to medium low and continue cooking the egg only until the white becomes opaque—about 2 minutes. Slide a spatula underneath and flip the egg-in-the-hole over to cook the top for 30 seconds to 1 minute.

Ta-da! Egg-in-the-Hole for 1.

French Toast

You can easily imagine how French toast was invented, can't you? Leftover bread, an egg, a little milk. It just happened.

1	egg
2 tbsp (30 ml)	milk
2 (or more) slices	bread, any kind, stale or fresh
1 tbsp (15 ml)	vegetable oil
	Cinnamon for sprinkling if desired

In a flattish bowl, beat together the egg with the milk. Dip the bread slices into this mixture, turning to coat both sides. Depending on the type of bread and size of the slices, you might have enough of the egg mixture to do more than 2 slices of bread. But maybe not.

Pour the oil in a small frying pan and place over medium heat. Lay the bread slices in the pan, sprinkle lightly with cinnamon (if you want) and cook until golden brown on one side. Turn, and cook the other side until golden brown, then remove to a plate.

Serve immediately with maple syrup, jam, cinnamon sugar, sliced strawberries or anything else that makes you happy.

Makes 1 serving—but feel free to double, triple, quadruple this recipe if needed.

 # Breakfast Burrito

Here's a great breakfast you can eat while you're hunting for your other shoe, trying to find the library book due today or even while running for the bus.

Warm a small flour tortilla in the microwave for 20 seconds or wrapped in foil in a 325°F (160°C) oven for about 10 minutes. Meanwhile, make some Basic Scrambled Eggs—the regular, frying pan, way or in the microwave (see page 21).

Scoop the scrambled eggs into the middle of the warm tortilla, top with some grated cheese, a spoonful of salsa (volcano-hot salsa is a real eye-opener first thing in the morning), some shredded lettuce (if you have some handy), chopped onions, green pepper—*whatever*. Fold up the bottom, roll in the two sides (leaving the top open) and away you go.

Pancakes Not from a Box

**Believe it or not, it's possible to make pancakes without a mix.
And it's not even hard.**

1¼ cups (300 ml)	all-purpose flour
1 tbsp (15 ml)	granulated sugar
1 tbsp (15 ml)	baking powder
1	egg
1 cup (250 ml)	milk
2 tbsp (30 ml)	vegetable oil
	Additional oil for the frying pan

In a medium-size bowl, stir together the flour, sugar and baking
powder. In another bowl, beat together the egg, milk and vegetable
oil. Add the egg mixture to the flour mixture and stir just until
combined—a few lumps don't matter.

Pour a small amount of vegetable oil into a large frying pan—just
enough to coat the surface with a film of oil. Place the frying pan over
medium heat and let it heat until a drop of water sizzles when you
sprinkle it in. Spoon about ¼ cup (50 ml) of the batter into the pan,
spreading it evenly. If the batter is too thick to pour easily, stir in a
little additional milk to thin it. Allow the pancake to cook on one side
until bubbles appear on the top, then flip it and let the other side cook
until golden. Remove to a plate and repeat with the remaining batter,
adding more oil to the frying pan as needed.

Once you get good at this, you can cook two or three pancakes at a
time.

Serve immediately with the usual accompaniments—and act casual
when people go crazy.

Makes about fourteen 4-inch (10 cm) pancakes.

Whole Wheat Blueberry Yogurt Pancakes

Eat these pancakes and you'll feel so healthy it's scary. If you don't want to feel quite so healthy, use a blend of whole wheat and white all-purpose flour. They're good either way.

1¼ cups (300 ml)	whole wheat flour
1 tbsp (15 ml)	granulated sugar
1 tsp (5 ml)	baking powder
½ tsp (2 ml)	baking soda
1¼ cups (300 ml)	plain yogurt, buttermilk or soured milk (see sidebar on page 27)
2 tbsp (30 ml)	vegetable oil
1	egg
1 cup (250 ml)	fresh or frozen blueberries
	Additional oil for the frying pan

In a medium bowl, combine the whole wheat flour, sugar, baking powder and baking soda. In another bowl, stir together the yogurt (or buttermilk or soured milk), oil, and egg. Add the buttermilk mixture to the flour mixture and stir just until combined. Gently fold in the blueberries. Don't overbeat this batter, because you'll deflate the fluffiness. (If the batter is too thick to pour easily, add up to ½ cup [125 ml] milk to thin it.)

Pour a small amount of vegetable oil into a large frying pan or griddle—just enough to coat the surface with a film of oil. Place the frying pan over medium heat and let it heat until a drop of water sizzles when you sprinkle it in. Spoon about ¼ cup (50 ml) of the batter into the pan, spreading it evenly. Allow the pancake to cook on one side until bubbles appear on the top, then flip it and let the other side cook until golden. The blueberries will leak juice as the pancakes cook—that's okay. Remove to a plate and repeat with the remaining batter, adding more oil to the frying pan as needed.

Serve immediately, or keep them warm on a plate in a 250°F (120°C) oven until all the pancakes are finished. Maple syrup is a must.

Makes about a dozen 4-inch (10 cm) pancakes.

Breakfast Pizza for One GF

Okay, so you can't quite bring yourself to just order a pizza for breakfast (do they even deliver at 7:30 a.m.?) and that cold slice from two days ago doesn't look so great anymore. Try this.

2 tsp (10 ml)	butter
2	eggs
¼ cup (50 ml)	spaghetti sauce
¼ cup (50 ml)	shredded mozzarella (or other) cheese
	Pepperoni, mushrooms, hot peppers, anchovies
	(any or all of the usual suspects)

Melt the butter in a small frying pan over medium heat. In a small bowl, beat the eggs and pour into the hot pan. Let the eggs cook just until the bottom is golden and the top has begun to set and is no longer completely runny. With a pancake turner, flip the eggs in the pan and right away spoon some spaghetti sauce onto the cooked side. Sprinkle with mozzarella cheese (and whatever else you're using) and cover the pan with a lid (or something—a plate will do). Let cook for a minute or two—just until the cheese melts.

Slide the pizza onto a plate, cut into wedges and eat.

Makes 1 serving. Repeat if necessary.

Making Soured Milk—and Why You'd Ever Want to Do Such a Thing

In the olden days before milk was routinely pasteurized, cooks used milk that had gone sour in breads, muffins or other baked goods. So you'll sometimes see recipes that call for soured milk. Sour milk (an acid) is used in combination with baking soda (a base) to provide a fun chemical reaction that causes bubbles to form—helpful for making baked things rise. But modern pasteurized milk doesn't sour in a nice, friendly way because the bacteria aren't the same as those in unpasteurized milk. Which means you'll have to cheat.

Cheat 1: Measure 1 tbsp (15 ml) of vinegar into a measuring cup. Fill the cup to the 1 cup (250 ml) mark with milk and stir. Let sit for about 5 minutes before using. The milk will go all icky and lumpy—exactly what you want. Congratulations! You have now made 1 cup (250 ml) of soured milk that you can use when you come across a recipe that calls for sour milk.

Cheat 2: Just substitute the same amount of commercial buttermilk for the sour milk in the recipe.

Cheat 3: Or use yogurt. Mix plain yogurt with just enough regular milk to make it pourable and use in any recipe that calls for sour milk or buttermilk.

Breakfast Smoothie GF EF

You've overslept. Again. If you're not out of the house in two minutes, you're in big trouble. What about breakfast? Here—drink this and run.

1 cup (250 ml)	cold milk
½ cup (125 ml)	plain or flavored yogurt
2 tbsp (30 ml)	orange juice concentrate (don't dilute)
1	Ripe banana, cut into chunks

Throw everything into the blender and let it zip while you tie your shoelaces.

Quick—into a glass—guzzle it down—and get going!

Makes 1 large serving (about 2 cups/500 ml).

Variation 1: Instead of the banana, substitute any fresh or frozen fruit: strawberries, blueberries, mangoes, peaches, raspberries—even a mix of two or three.

Variation 2: Use your favorite fruit juice instead of milk in the recipe above.

Salads, Soups and Side Things

Coleslaw GF EF DF

The world's cheapest and easiest salad. One head of cabbage makes a ton of coleslaw, and if made with Sweet and Sour Coleslaw Dressing, it will keep in the fridge for as long as a week. (Coleslaw with creamy dressing, on the other hand, is best eaten soon after it's been made.)

½	small head of cabbage (about 6 cups shredded)
2	green onions, chopped
1	carrot, grated
1	green pepper, chopped
1	apple, chopped (optional)
½ cup (125 ml)	raisins (optional)

Combine all the shredded and chopped ingredients in a large bowl. Toss with either Creamy Coleslaw Dressing or Sweet and Sour Coleslaw Dressing (pages 37–38). If you're using apples or raisins in your coleslaw, the creamy dressing is especially delicious—but you'll be the judge of that, won't you?

Makes 8 to 10 servings.

 **The Best Potato Salad** GF DF

Even better than your mom's. But don't tell her that.

4 or 5	medium potatoes, scrubbed but not peeled
2 tbsp (30 ml)	apple cider vinegar or white wine vinegar
2 tbsp (30 ml)	water
½ tsp (2 ml)	salt
¼ tsp (1 ml)	black pepper
1	small onion, chopped
1 stalk	celery, diced
1 or 2	hard-boiled eggs, peeled and chopped (see page 20)
2 tbsp (30 ml)	chopped fresh parsley
½ cup (125 ml)	mayonnaise

First, cook your potatoes. In a medium saucepan, cover the potatoes with water, bring to a boil over medium-high heat and cook until tender but not mushy. (If you prefer, steam them in a steamer basket over boiling water.) This will take 20 to 35 minutes, depending on the type of potato. To check for doneness, poke a knife into a potato—it should slide right in without hitting a hard spot. Drain, then let the potatoes cool just until you can handle them easily.

Peel the potatoes (if they're done, the skins will come off easily) and cut them into ½-inch (1 cm) cubes. Place in a medium-size bowl.

In a small bowl, mix the vinegar, water, salt and pepper and toss with the potato cubes, being careful not to mush them up. Refrigerate until completely cool.

Add the rest of the ingredients—the onion, celery, eggs, parsley and mayonnaise—and toss until everything is well mixed. Chill thoroughly before serving.

Makes about 4 servings.

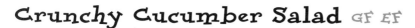

Crunchy Cucumber Salad GF EF

When lettuce is $2 a head and tomatoes are as tough as tennis balls, you can still have a salad with dinner.

½ cup (125 ml)	white wine vinegar (or regular white vinegar)
½ cup (125 ml)	water
1 tbsp (15 ml)	sugar
2	large seedless cucumbers, peeled and thinly sliced (about 3 cups/750 ml)
	Salt and pepper to taste
	Sour cream if desired

In a medium bowl, combine the vinegar, water and sugar. Add the cucumber slices to the dressing, toss well and refrigerate until serving time.

When you're ready to eat, drain the cucumber slices into a bowl, sprinkle with salt and pepper to taste and a little chopped fresh (or dried) dill if you have it. Add a dollop of sour cream if you like that kind of thing.

Makes 3 or 4 servings.

Chunky Pasta Salad

Pasta salad was invented to take care of leftovers. A bit of pasta, some slivers of red pepper, a few cooked green beans, half an onion, a forgotten hunk of cheese—that sort of thing. Throw it all into a bowl, add some dressing and you've made something out of nothing.

2 cups (500 ml)	uncooked rotini or other medium-size pasta shape (or 3 cups/750 ml leftover cooked pasta)
1 tsp (5 ml)	olive or vegetable oil
3 cups (750 ml)	(total amount) mixed diced cooked and raw vegetables, cheese, ham, cooked chicken, salami, canned chickpeas or beans (or see below for more ideas)
¼ cup (50 ml)	mayonnaise
¼ cup (50 ml)	plain yogurt
2 tsp (10 ml)	apple cider vinegar or other vinegar
1 clove	fresh garlic, minced (or ¼ tsp/1 ml garlic powder)
½ tsp (2 ml)	salt
¼ tsp (1 ml)	black pepper

If you're starting with raw pasta, bring a large pot of water to a boil, add the pasta and cook on high heat until the pasta is tender but not at all mushy. Drain in a colander, then rinse under cold running water. Place in a large bowl and toss with the oil to help keep the pasta from sticking together. If you're using leftover pasta, just rinse with cold water to remove surface stickiness, then toss in a bowl with the oil.

Add all the vegetables and whatever other chunky bits you're putting in the salad (the chicken, cheese, beans and so on). If you're not serving the salad right away, cover with plastic wrap and refrigerate until ready to serve.

In a small bowl, whisk together the mayonnaise, yogurt, vinegar, garlic or garlic powder, salt and pepper. Just before serving, pour over the salad and toss well to coat everything with dressing. Don't add the dressing too far ahead of time, because the pasta will soak it up like a sponge. Sample, and adjust the seasoning to your taste.

If there's any salad left over, refrigerate it and toss with additional dressing before serving.

Makes 3 or 4 servings.

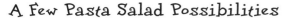

A Few Pasta Salad Possibilities

- defrosted frozen peas, corn or edamame (green soy beans)
- chopped green onion
- crumbled feta cheese
- sliced olives
- diced avocado
- chopped red onion
- slivered fresh basil
- cooked or grilled turkey, sausage, beef or pork
- hot pepper rings
- lightly steamed broccoli, cauliflower, snow peas

Multibean Salad GF EF DF

Colorful, tasty and cheap! It's all good.

3 cans (19 oz/540 ml each)	any kind of beans—kidney beans, chickpeas, black beans, mixed beans
1	medium yellow or red onion, diced
1	medium sweet green, red or yellow pepper, diced
1	medium tomato, diced (or 1 cup/250 ml cherry or grape tomatoes, halved)
¼ cup (50 ml)	chopped fresh parsley
½ cup (125 ml)	olive or vegetable oil
⅓ cup (75 ml)	cider vinegar or other vinegar
1 clove	garlic, minced or pressed
2 tbsp (30 ml)	granulated sugar
1 tsp (5 ml)	salt
½ tsp (2 ml)	black pepper

Open the cans of beans and dump them into a strainer or colander. Rinse under cold running water, drain well and transfer to a large mixing bowl. Add the diced onion and pepper, the tomatoes and parsley.

In a small bowl, whisk together the oil, vinegar, garlic, sugar, salt and pepper. Pour this dressing over the bean mixture and toss well to mix. Cover with plastic wrap and chill in the refrigerator for about 1 hour to let the ingredients get to know one another. Just before serving, toss again to mix.

Makes 6 to 8 servings.

Great Antipasto

Antipasto is a work of art. A symphony. Well, maybe that's a little much. Anyway, it's not meat loaf—although there could be meat loaf in it. Or practically anything else, for that matter. It can consist of three or four well-chosen and delicious items arranged on a plate or it can be a wild collection of odds and ends. It can be an appetizer or it can be dinner. And the nicest thing about it is that you don't actually have to cook anything.

Some of the following items you can find at an Italian grocery; some you can pick up from your supermarket deli. Some things are fresh and others come out of cans or jars. Use your imagination— express yourself in your antipasto:

- marinated artichoke hearts
- sliced provolone or other cheese
- anchovies
- olives—green, black, wrinkled, spicy, stuffed, unstuffed
- thinly sliced Italian salami, ham or prosciutto
- bocconcini (little balls of fresh mozzarella cheese)
- canned sardines
- pickled peppers
- marinated mushrooms
- cherry tomatoes
- roasted red peppers or eggplant
- sun-dried tomatoes (packed in oil with herbs)
- canned tuna
- hard-boiled egg wedges
- celery and carrot sticks

Arrange your chosen antipasto components decoratively on a platter— roll up the cheese and sliced meat, make a face with the olives, garnish everything with a pickled pepper or two—you know the sort of thing. Serve with a warm loaf of crusty Italian bread (if you happen to find fresh focaccia or ciabatta, grab it).

Buon appetito!

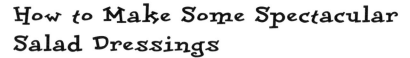

How to Make Some Spectacular Salad Dressings

You can (and should) make your own salad dressing. It costs next to nothing, takes about 5 minutes to mix and will be better tasting and fresher than anything you can buy in a store.

Basic Vinaigrette Dressing EF DF

You can use this no-nonsense dressing as is, or make it the start of a more elaborate concoction. Use olive oil if you have it (or whatever oil you do have in the house) and any type of vinegar you want. Experiment with different oils and vinegars (see below for suggestions). Add fresh or dried herbs, spices, grated cheese, garlic, ketchup, mustard—mess around with this basic recipe and see where it goes.

¾ cup (175 ml)	oil (see below)
¼ cup (50 ml)	vinegar (see below)
1 tbsp (15 ml)	Dijon mustard (optional)
	Salt and pepper to taste

In a small bowl, whisk the ingredients together until thoroughly mixed. Taste, and adjust salt and pepper if needed. If you're using the Dijon mustard, the dressing will remain mixed (technically speaking, emulsified). Otherwise, the oil and vinegar will eventually separate. No big deal—just rewhisk if necessary.

Makes about 1 cup (250 ml)—enough for a large salad. You can keep leftover dressing in the fridge practically forever.

Oil variations

- olive
- canola
- sunflower
- grape seed
- peanut
- corn
- walnut
- sesame
- vegetable, which may be soy oil or a combination of several kinds of oils

Vinegar variations

- apple cider vinegar
- white vinegar
- balsamic vinegar
- red wine and white wine vinegar
- sherry vinegar
- rice wine vinegar (or try lemon juice instead)

Creamy Italian Dressing DF

Start with a Basic Vinaigrette Dressing, then add some stuff and turn it into Creamy Italian. Just like that.

1 recipe	Basic Vinaigrette Dressing, preferably made with olive oil (see page 35)
¼ cup (50 ml)	mayonnaise
1 clove	garlic, minced or pressed
½ tsp (2 ml)	crumbled dried oregano
¼ tsp (1 ml)	crumbled dried thyme
	Salt and pepper to taste

In a small bowl, whisk the ingredients together until thoroughly mixed. Taste, and adjust seasoning if necessary.

Makes about 1 cup (250 ml) of dressing—enough for a large salad. Leftovers will keep in the fridge for a week.

 # Slightly Caesar Dressing

Another Basic Vinaigrette variation. See—isn't it useful?

1 recipe	Basic Vinaigrette Dressing (see page 35)
¼ cup (50 ml)	mayonnaise
1 clove	garlic (or more), minced or pressed
1 tbsp (5 ml)	Dijon mustard
1 tsp (5 ml)	Worcestershire sauce
2 tbsp (30 ml)	grated Parmesan cheese (or more, to taste)
1 or 2	minced canned anchovies (a classic touch, but optional)
	Salt and pepper to taste

Whisk the Basic Vinaigrette Dressing and the mayonnaise until well mixed. Add the garlic, mustard, Worcestershire sauce, Parmesan cheese and anchovies (if you're using them), and whisk again until smooth. Taste, and add salt and pepper, if you think the dressing needs it.

Makes a little more than 1 cup (250 ml). Leftover dressing can be refrigerated for 2 or 3 days.

Desperation Ranch Dressing GF DF

Desperation can be the mother of invention.

½ cup (125 ml) mayonnaise
¼ cup (50 ml) dill (or other) pickle juice

Mix the mayonnaise and the pickle juice, adjusting the seasoning, if necessary, until the dressing tastes right. You can use the juice from any kind of pickle for this recipe, but most experts recommend dill pickle juice.

Makes ¾ cup (175 ml)—enough for a couple of big salads. Leftover dressing keeps well in the fridge.

Zorba the Greek Dressing GF EF DF

Singing, dancing and plate smashing are optional.

½ cup (125 ml) olive oil
3 tbsp (45 ml) lemon juice
1 tsp (5 ml) crumbled dried oregano
Salt and pepper

In a small bowl, whisk together all the ingredients until combined.

Use this dressing on a Greek salad of romaine lettuce with tomato, cucumber, black olives, red onion and crumbled feta cheese.

Makes ¾ cup (175 ml)—enough for a large Greek salad. You can keep the leftover dressing in the fridge for about a week.

Creamy Coleslaw Dressing GF

½ cup (125 ml) mayonnaise
½ cup (125 ml) plain yogurt
Salt, black pepper and a pinch of sugar (if you want)

In a small bowl, stir together the mayonnaise and yogurt until blended. Season with salt and pepper—and a pinch of sugar if the mixture is too tart for your delicate taste buds.

Makes 1 cup (250 ml) of dressing—enough for a very large bowl of coleslaw. Leftover dressing doesn't keep very well, so only make as much as you can use right away.

Sweet and Sour Coleslaw Dressing GF EF DF

½ cup (125 ml)	vegetable oil or olive oil
⅓ cup (75 ml)	apple cider vinegar or other vinegar
1 tbsp (15 ml)	granulated sugar
1 tsp (5 ml)	celery seeds
	Salt and black pepper to taste

Whisk all the ingredients together in a small bowl.

Makes about 1 cup (250 ml) of dressing—enough for a large bowl of coleslaw. Refrigerated, coleslaw made with this type of dressing will keep very nicely for several days. If anything, it's even better the next day.

What Is a Garlic Clove—and How Do You Chop It?

When a recipe calls for a clove of garlic, it means *one section* of the bulb. If the recipe calls for a head of garlic (we're talking *serious* garlic here), you'll be using the *whole bulb*.

Some recipes ask you to *chop, mince* or *press* a clove of garlic. Here's a quick, violent method to do the job: place the clove on a chopping board, yell "HAYAH!" and whack the garlic firmly with the side of a broad knife or cleaver. The skin will peel off, and the garlic clove will be mostly in pieces. Remove the bits of skin. A few additional chops and you're done. Very effective—and fun.

Or else you can use a garlic press. Your choice.

How to Chop an Onion Without Crying

Amaze your friends and family with this spectacular trick! Place your cutting board over the *front* burner of the stove. (Do not turn it on!) Pay attention here—this is critical—turn the *back* burner on high. The back burner gets turned *on*—the front burner is *off*. Got that? Now place your onion on the cutting board (which is sitting on the *front* burner) and chop away to your heart's content. For complex scientific reasons, the heat from the back burner of the stove attracts the tear-producing onion vapors and draws them away from your delicate eyeballs. Unbelievable but true. Just *please* don't forget to turn that stove burner off when you're finished chopping. And, of course, take a bow. Ta-da!

A scuba mask also works—but isn't quite as awesome.

How to Chop Any Vegetable

Obviously, vegetables don't want to be chopped. Or so it would seem. In a desperate attempt to avoid being minced, most vegetables are inconveniently shaped. They have round sides. They have uneven bumps. They have pits. But these strategies cannot save them from our superior intellect!

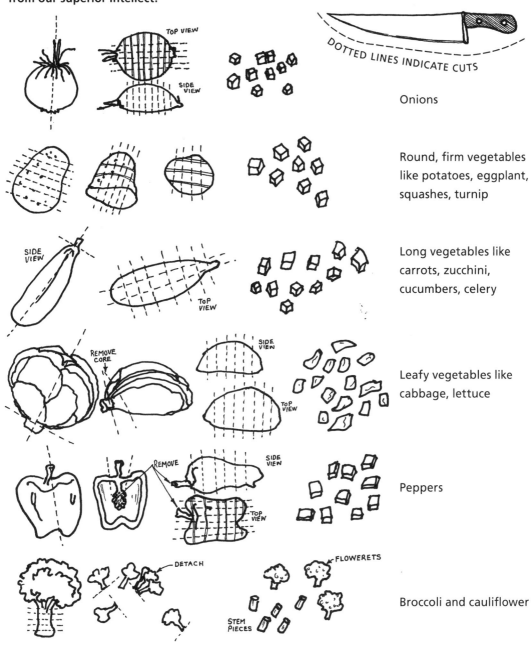

DOTTED LINES INDICATE CUTS

Onions

Round, firm vegetables like potatoes, eggplant, squashes, turnip

Long vegetables like carrots, zucchini, cucumbers, celery

Leafy vegetables like cabbage, lettuce

Peppers

Broccoli and cauliflower

Soups

Potato Soup GF EF

A loaf of bread, a big bowl of potato soup—what more do you need? Okay. Maybe a car.

2	medium onions, chopped
2 cloves	garlic, minced or pressed
2 tbsp (30 ml)	butter, olive oil or vegetable oil
4	large potatoes, peeled and cubed (about 3 cups/750 ml cubed)
4 cups (1 l)	chicken or vegetable broth (prepared broth or made from bouillon cubes or powder)
2 cups (500 ml)	milk
½ tsp (2 ml)	salt
¼ tsp (1 ml)	black pepper

In a large pot, sauté the onions and garlic in the butter or oil over medium heat for 3 to 5 minutes, or just until softened. Add the potatoes and the broth and bring to a boil. Cover the pot and simmer for 15 to 20 minutes, or until the potatoes are squishy and completely tender when poked with a fork.

For a smooth and creamy soup, pour into a blender or food processor (do this in batches) and blend until smooth, then return to the pot. (If you have an immersion blender—sometimes called a stick blender—you can puree right in the cooking pot.) Otherwise, for a more rustic look, you can just mash the whole business with a fork or potato masher. Either way, add the milk, salt and pepper, place over medium-low heat and let the soup heat through without boiling.

Makes 4 to 6 servings.

Cool French variation

Prepare the soup as above, then chill thoroughly. Serve cold, sprinkled with chopped chives or green onions and call it vichyssoise. You may have to thin it with a bit more milk if the soup has thickened in the fridge. For extra bonus points, use 2 chopped leeks instead of the onions in the recipe.

Pumpkin Soup GF EF DF

Few sights are more pathetic than a shriveled old pumpkin the day after Halloween. Don't allow your jack-o'-lantern to die in vain. Make this soup.

2 tbsp (30 ml)	butter, olive oil or vegetable oil
1	onion, chopped
4 cups (1 l)	peeled, cubed, raw pumpkin (or squash—see below)
2	medium potatoes, peeled and cubed (1½ cups/375 ml)
4 cups (1 l)	chicken or vegetable broth (prepared broth or made from bouillon cubes or powder)
1 tsp (5 ml)	salt
½ tsp (2 ml)	curry powder if desired
¼ tsp (1 ml)	black pepper

In a large pot, sauté the onions in the butter or oil over medium heat for about 5 minutes, or just until softened. Add the pumpkin and the potato, and stir for a minute or so. Pour in the broth, cover and bring to a boil, stirring occasionally. Let the mixture cook until the pumpkin and potato are really soft when poked with a fork—about 30 minutes.

If you want a smooth and creamy soup, pour the soup into a blender or food processor (in batches) and blend until smooth, then return to the pot. (If you have an immersion—stick—blender, you can puree right in the cooking pot.) Or you can just mash the whole business up with a potato masher. The masher method is a little less elegant, but just as tasty. Return the soup to the pot to heat through, adding a little more broth or a splash of milk if it seems too thick— some pumpkins and squash are more watery than others. Season with salt and pepper (and a little curry powder if you're the type) and serve.

Makes 4 to 6 servings.

Squash options

If pumpkins aren't available, you can make this soup with any winter squash. Look for butternut, hubbard, turban, buttercup or kabocha squash—cut in half, scoop out the seeds, peel and use exactly as if it were a pumpkin.

Spinach Soup EF

Sometimes you just need something green.

2 pkgs (10 oz/285 g each)	fresh spinach
2 tbsp (30 ml)	butter, olive oil or vegetable oil
1	small onion, finely chopped
2 tbsp (30 ml)	all-purpose flour
4 cups (1 l)	milk, divided (see below)
1 tsp (5 ml)	salt
¼ tsp (1 ml)	black pepper
¼ tsp (1 ml)	nutmeg if desired

Rinse the spinach under running water, pick out the weird wilted bits and anything that doesn't look like spinach and dump it into a pot. Pack the spinach down into the pot so that it all fits. Don't add any more water than what is left clinging to the leaves after washing. Cover with a lid and cook over medium heat, stirring from time to time, until the spinach has completely wilted and shrunk into a sorry-looking mass in the bottom of the pot. Dump the spinach and all the liquid that has seeped out into a blender, add 2 cups (500 ml) of the milk (*half* the total amount of milk) and blend until smooth.

In the same pot that you cooked the spinach (don't bother washing the pot—it'll be fine) sauté the onion in the butter or oil over medium heat for about 5 minutes, or just until soft. Add the flour, stir well, then pour in the remaining 2 cups (500 ml) of the milk. Gently bring this to a simmer, stirring often, until the liquid begins to bubble and thickens slightly. Pour in the blended spinach mixture, stir well and allow to just heat through (don't let it boil). Season with salt and pepper and sprinkle each serving with a little nutmeg (if you like that sort of thing).

Makes 4 to 6 servings.

X-Ray Vision Soup GF EF DF

This soup is so full of carrots that after you eat a bowlful, you'll be able to see right through walls. Not to mention clothing. Lead-lined underwear is recommended for bashful eaters.

2 tbsp (30 ml)	butter, olive oil or vegetable oil
1	medium onion, chopped
3 cups (750 ml)	scrubbed and coarsely shredded carrots (about 3 medium carrots)
¼ tsp (1 ml)	turmeric (if you have it)
4 cups (1 l)	chicken or vegetable broth (prepared broth or made from bouillon cubes or powder)
½ tsp (2 ml)	Italian seasoning (or a pinch each dried oregano, thyme and basil)
1 cup (250 ml)	corn kernels (fresh, frozen or canned)
1 tsp (5 ml)	salt
tsp (1 ml)	black pepper

Heat the butter or oil in a large saucepan over medium heat. Add the chopped onions and sauté just until softened—3 to 5 minutes. Add the shredded carrots and the turmeric, and cook, stirring occasionally, until carrots are wilted. (The turmeric is there to really amp up the color, but if you don't have any, just leave it out.)

Stir in the broth and Italian seasoning, bring to a boil over medium high heat and simmer, covered, for 10 minutes. Add the corn, salt and pepper, and cook for another 5 minutes or so.

Makes 6 to 8 servings.

Garbage Broth—It's Free!

Celery leaves. Parsley stems. Green pepper insides. Chicken bones. Rubbery carrots. Meat trimmings. You weren't planning to throw that stuff away, were you? Of course not. What looks like garbage to the untrained eye is actually the makings of a flavorful broth. Just toss all these bits and pieces—vegetable trimmings, wilted leaves, cores, stems—into a plastic bag in the freezer. When you've saved up enough of this junk to fill a pot, add water to cover and simmer until the cows come home. You may have to throw in some extra seasonings for flavor—salt, pepper, herbs and spices—but eventually, your concoction will turn into something brothy and worthwhile. Strain out the solids and use it as a base for soup.

Mushroom Barley Soup EF DF

This old-fashioned homey soup is perfect on a stormy day when you need a little comfort food.

2 tbsp (30 ml)	butter, olive oil or vegetable oil
2	small onions, chopped
2	medium carrots, chopped
1 stalk	celery, chopped
2 cloves	garlic, squished
1 lb (500 g)	mushrooms, sliced
3 quarts (3 l)	chicken or vegetable broth (prepared broth or made from bouillon cubes or powder)
¾ cup (175 ml)	uncooked pearl barley
1 tsp (5 ml)	dried thyme
1 tsp (5 ml)	salt
¼ tsp (1 ml)	black pepper
2 tbsp (30 ml)	chopped fresh parsley

In a large pot or Dutch oven, heat the butter or oil over medium heat. Add the onions, carrots, celery and garlic, and cook, stirring, for about 10 minutes, or until the vegetables are beginning to get tender. Add the sliced mushrooms and let cook for another 5 to 8 minutes, or until the mushrooms have released their juices (wait for it!), then continue to cook, stirring, for 2 or 3 minutes more.

Now add the broth, barley, thyme, salt and pepper, and bring to a boil over medium-high heat. Cover the pot with a lid, lower the heat to medium low and let the soup cook, stirring occasionally, for 1 to 1½ hours, until the barley is completely tender. If the soup is becoming too thick, add a bit more broth (or even just water) to thin it. Add the chopped parsley and simmer for another 5 to 10 minutes.

Makes 8 to 10 servings.

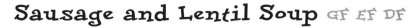

Sausage and Lentil Soup GF EF DF

A full meal in a soup—in less than half an hour. You can do this.

1 tbsp (15 ml)	olive or vegetable oil
1	medium onion, chopped
2 cloves	garlic, minced or pressed
1	medium carrot, chopped
1 stalk	celery, chopped
1 tsp (5 ml)	ground cumin
1 can (28 oz/796 ml)	diced tomatoes
1 can (19 oz/540 ml)	lentils, drained
2 cups (500 ml)	chicken or vegetable broth (prepared broth or made from bouillon cubes or powder)
½ lb (250 g)	kielbasa or any smoked sausage, cut into ½-inch (1 cm) cubes
½ tsp (2 ml)	salt
¼ tsp (1 ml)	black pepper

Heat the oil in a large saucepan or Dutch oven over medium heat, add the onion, garlic, carrot, celery and cumin, and cook, stirring once in a while, until the vegetables are soft and beginning to brown—about 10 minutes.

Add the diced tomatoes, the lentils and the broth, and bring to a boil. Reduce the heat to medium low, cover and let the soup simmer for about 15 minutes, or until the vegetables are tender. Add the sausage, salt and pepper, and continue to cook for another 5 minutes, or until heated through.

Serve with some good bread, and ta-da!

Makes about 4 servings.

Vegetarian alert

Omit the sausage, use vegetable broth as the cooking liquid and double the lentils for a hearty vegetarian version of this soup.

Turkey Aftermath Soup DF

It's the day after Thanksgiving, Christmas or whatever. A turkey carcass lurks in the fridge, daring you to deal with it. Don't be scared—make this easy and delicious soup.

1	turkey carcass—the picked-over bones of a roast turkey (plus any leftover skin, gravy, meat scraps and so on)
8 to 10 cups (2 to 2.5 l)	cold water (or enough to cover)
2	carrots, peeled and sliced
1	medium onion, chopped
2 stalks	celery, sliced
	Salt and pepper to taste
1 cup (250 ml)	uncooked medium-width noodles

By hand (wear clean rubber gloves if you're squeamish), break up the turkey carcass into manageable hunks and place in a pot large enough to hold it, along with any bits of roasted skin you might have hanging around. Add the water, carrots, onion and celery, and bring to a boil over medium-high heat. Cover, reduce heat to medium low and let this concoction simmer for 1 to 1½ hours. Taste the broth, and adjust the seasoning with salt and pepper if needed.

Place a colander or large strainer over another large saucepan. Strain the broth and discard the bones and skin, but hang on to the vegetables as best you can (a messy business, for sure).

Return the veggies to the broth, along with any bits of meat and gravy that might be left over. Add the uncooked noodles, bring to a boil over medium-high heat and cook just until the noodles are tender.

Makes 4 to 6 servings.

Does Your Soup Need a Boost?

If the broth tastes wishy-washy, maybe not enough flavor remained on those turkey bones to make a tasty stock. Luckily, you can fix this. Add a spoonful or two of bouillon powder (or a couple of cubes) to give the soup a bit more flavor. You can also throw in any other veggies—cooked, raw or frozen—you might have hanging around. It's your soup and you're the boss of it.

Classic Chicken Soup GF EF DF

It started as a scratchy throat. Then you got a stuffy nose and a headache. And now—uh-oh—you're coughing. Make some chicken soup, wrap yourself in a blankie and eat your soup in front of the TV. Maybe you'll catch your favorite *Simpsons* episode. Again.

5 lbs (2.5 kg)	cheap chicken parts (necks, backs, legs, thighs, whatever is on sale)
1	large onion, chopped
4 stalks	celery, cut into chunks
4	large carrots, cut into chunks
3 cloves	garlic, peeled but left whole
1 handful	fresh parsley, washed
8 to 10 cups (2 to 2.5 l)	cold water (or enough to cover)
2 tsp (10 ml)	salt
1 tsp (5 ml)	black pepper

Rinse the chicken pieces under running water and put into a large pot. Add the onion, celery, carrots, garlic and parsley, and pour in enough cold water to cover everything with about an inch (2 cm) or so to spare. Bring to a boil over medium heat, then lower the heat to a simmer. Let cook, partly covered (leave the cover slightly ajar to prevent a boil-over), for at least 2 hours. Or longer, if you have the time.

Add the salt and pepper after the soup has been cooking for about 1 hour. At the end of the cooking time, taste the broth and adjust the seasoning. (If you have a cold, remember that your taste buds are shot, so have someone taste it for you.)

Place a strainer or colander over another large pot and strain the soup completely. Let cool slightly and, with a large spoon, skim as much of the fat (the clear, yellowish, floaty stuff) off the top as possible and discard it. (Neat trick—if you're not in a big hurry for your soup, refrigerate the broth overnight, then you can just scoop the congealed fat off the top easily.) Pick any meat off the bones, cut up the carrots and the celery and throw everything back into the broth. If you want noodles or rice (and who wouldn't?), cook them separately in boiling water until tender before adding to the chicken soup.

There you go. Chicken soup that will make you feel *much* better if you're sick, but can also be safely consumed by a perfectly healthy person.

Makes about 2 quarts (2 l).

Minestrone Soup EF DF

Old Italian Minestrone Soup Secret: If you grate your own Parmesan cheese, save the rinds and toss a couple of hunks into the soup as it cooks. Fish them out of the pot before serving.

2 tbsp (30 ml)	olive oil or vegetable oil
2	medium onions, chopped
2	cloves garlic, minced or pressed
1	carrot, sliced ¼ inch (.5 cm) thick
2 stalks	celery, sliced ¼ inch (.5 cm) thick
1 can (28 oz/796 ml)	diced tomatoes
4 cups (1 l)	water
½ cup (125 ml)	any small pasta shape, uncooked (like tiny shells, tubes or alphabets)
1 cup (250 ml)	green beans, cut crosswise into ½-inch (1 cm) pieces
2	small zucchini, sliced ¼ inch (.5 cm) thick
3 cups (750 ml)	raw spinach, roughly torn up
1 can (19 oz/540 ml)	red or white kidney beans, rinsed and drained
½ tsp (2 ml)	salt
¼ tsp (1 ml)	black pepper
	Grated Parmesan cheese for serving if desired

Before you begin, take some time to chop, dice and slice everything you need for the soup. Once you start cooking, you'll be glad it's all ready to go.

Heat the oil in a large pot over medium heat. Add the onions and garlic, and sauté for about 5 minutes, or until softened. Add the carrot, celery, tomatoes and water. (If you have any Parmesan cheese rinds, add them now.) Bring to a boil, then reduce the heat to low, cover the pot and simmer, stirring occasionally, for about 40 minutes—just long enough to clean up the mess in the kitchen. Almost.

Now add the uncooked pasta and the green beans, and cook for 10 minutes. Finally, add the zucchini, spinach and canned beans, and continue to cook for another 10 to 20 minutes. Season with salt and pepper. Pass around grated Parmesan cheese at the table to sprinkle on each serving, if desired.

Makes about 10 servings.

Onion Soup au Gratin EF

**You are sitting in a leetle bistro weeth a *personne très spéciale.*
Le garçon brings you *la soupe.* You *mange. Très romantique,
n'est-ce pas?***

2 tbsp (30 ml)	butter, olive oil or vegetable oil
4	medium onions, thinly sliced
6 cups (1.5 l)	beef broth (use a good brand of prepared broth)
	Salt and black pepper to taste
4	thick slices French or Italian bread, toasted
1 cup (250 ml)	grated Swiss or Gruyère cheese

In a medium saucepan, heat the butter or oil over medium-low heat.
Add the onions and s-l-o-w-l-y sauté them until golden brown and
caramelized. This will take longer than you expect—maybe 30 to
40 minutes or more. Don't try to rush it. Add the broth and simmer,
covered, for about 20 minutes. Taste, and add salt and pepper if
needed, but take it easy, because prepared broth can be pretty salty
already.

When you're ready to serve, turn the oven broiler to high and let
it preheat for a few minutes. Arrange 4 ovenproof bowls on a cookie
sheet or baking pan and ladle the soup into them. Float a slice of
toasted bread in each bowl of soup and sprinkle the cheese evenly over
them. Place under the preheated broiler and broil just until the cheese
melts and gets bubbly—*don't leave the room* while this is happening,
because the toasted cheese can go from perfect to cremated in less than
a minute.

Voilà—parfait, n'est-ce pas?

Unfortunately, this makes 4 servings, so you'll have to invite
another couple. Sorry.

Vegetarian alert

Use a good brand of prepared vegetable broth instead of beef broth for
a vegetarian version of this soup—the flavor will be slightly different,
but the soup will still be *très délicieuse!*

Gazpacho GF EF DF

Look! In your bowl! Is it a soup? Is it a salad? On a hot summer day, who really cares? It's great. Make sure to use good, flavorful, in-season tomatoes for this.

3 cloves	garlic, minced or pressed
4	ripe tomatoes
4 cups (1 l)	tomato juice or tomato-vegetable juice, divided (see below)
6	green onions, cut into chunks
2 stalks	celery, cut into chunks
2	medium cucumbers, peeled and diced
1	sweet green pepper, seeded and diced
1	small fresh hot pepper, seeded and diced (very optional)
¼ cup (50 ml)	lemon juice or white wine vinegar
1 tsp (5 ml)	salt
½ tsp (2 ml)	pepper
	Sour cream or plain yogurt for serving if desired
	Finely chopped parsley or chives for serving if desired

In the container of a blender or food processor, combine the garlic, 2 of the tomatoes and about half the tomato juice, and blend until smooth. Add the green onions, celery, cucumbers, green pepper and hot pepper, and blend—with quick on/off pulses—just so the vegetables are coarsely chopped. This mixture should stay quite chunky. Transfer gazpacho to a large mixing bowl. Stir in the remaining tomato juice, lemon juice or vinegar and salt and pepper. Chop the remaining 2 tomatoes coarsely and add to the soup. Taste, and adjust seasoning if needed. Chill for at least 1 hour if possible.

To serve, ladle the gazpacho into bowls, swirl in a small blob of sour cream or yogurt and sprinkle with parsley or chives. Or just serve it plain. Either way it's great.

Makes about 6 servings.

How to Make a Great Sandwich

Oh sure, you can slap a slice of baloney between two slices of white bread and call it a sandwich. And technically, it is. But is it a *great* sandwich? Not likely. A great sandwich is a creation. It is a thing of beauty. And besides, it goes so well with a bowl of soup.

1. *The bread is the main thing.* It should be fresh, and it should have *character.* Look for whole grain bread, crusty bread, bread with cheese in it. Try a chewy rye bread, or a roasted garlic loaf, or a rustic Italian ciabatta. Whatever. Even slightly stale bread can work if you toast it.

2. *The filling.* Rummage through the fridge to find a forgotten treasure. A single, lonely piece of leftover chicken. Cold meat loaf. Some stinky cheese. A hard-boiled egg. Baked beans. Avoid anything green and furry.

3. *Accessories.* Lettuce, tomato, onion, hot peppers, arugula. What about some olives? Or leftover coleslaw? Pickles? Anchovies? Don't be shy—it's only a sandwich.

4. *The assembly.* First, waterproof the bread. Butter works nicely and so does mayonnaise. How about a mixture of mayonnaise and mustard? Or cheese spread, or hamburger relish, or peanut butter, or barbecue sauce. There has to be *something* interesting in the fridge. Next, layer on your filling ingredients and accessories. Invent a totally weird combination and see how it tastes. Elvis liked peanut butter and onion with mayonnaise. Yum.

5. *To toast or not to toast?* That *is* the question. If not, just proceed to step 6. If yes, place the finished sandwich on a frying pan or griddle over medium heat (lightly butter the outsides if you want). Press on the sandwich with a spatula, and toast, turning over once, until both sides are lightly browned and the innards are warm and melty in a good way.

6. Cut your fabulous sandwich in half (diagonally? in quarters? squares?), and after taking a moment to admire your creation—*eat it.*

   Elvis would be proud. Or jealous.

Pita Pockets

Pita bread is a wonderful thing. You can stuff almost anything into it. Rummage through the refrigerator to find odds and ends of leftovers, bits of lettuce, tomato, cheese, a few shreds of chicken (see page 51, step 2). None of these is enough to really make a meal, but together they are transcendent (look it up).

Begin with the right kind of pita. You want the type that has a pocket—Greek-style pita doesn't open into a pocket, so check the label on the bag. The pita must be very fresh. Stale pita will crumble and crack and refuse to cooperate. Cut the pita into two even halves (to make two pockets), or slice about one-quarter off the top (to make one giant pocket). Carefully spread the sides apart, trying not to tear the bread.

Next, you have to leak-proof the pocket. Professionals recommend lining your pita with some sort of shredded green stuff. Lettuce or cabbage is very effective for this. Gently jam this material down to the bottom of the pita.

Now plunk in whatever treasures you've found. Grated cheese, chopped tomato, cucumber, onion, sliced meat or fish, canned beans, tuna, salmon—anything at all. Experiment with weird and wonderful combinations of ingredients.

Drizzle in a little salad dressing, mayonnaise (thinned with pickle juice), salsa, barbecue sauce, tahini—anything—sprinkle with salt and pepper, and eat.

Okay, so it leaks a little. Catch the drips with a napkin.

Wrap It Up

Making a wrap is a delicate art. Here is a step-by-step guide to help you create the perfect one.

1. Begin with a large, fresh flour tortilla about 10 inches (25 cm) in diameter. You can use white or whole wheat, or one of the fancy kinds made with spinach or sun-dried tomato or whatever. Lay your chosen tortilla flat on a plate or cutting board.
2. Spread the tortilla with something that will act as the "glue." Mayonnaise, butter, peanut butter, cream cheese, refried beans—a thin layer only—right to the edges.
3. Now for the filling. Where to start? Sliced or diced meat or fish; veggies of all sorts— shredded lettuce, chopped red onion, diced tomatoes, grated carrots, sliced avocado; cheese, of course—shredded cheddar, mozzarella or Monterey Jack, crumbled feta or goat cheese, sliced Swiss; beans, hard-cooked egg, leftover Chinese takeout. They're all good. Pile filling ingredients in the middle of the tortilla, in a sort of elongated stack, leaving the edges clear. Don't overdo it or you'll have a hard time rolling the wrap.
4. To wrap the wrap, fold the sides of the tortilla in over the filling and then firmly roll from bottom to top to enclose everything, with the glue holding it together. If you aren't planning to eat this immediately, wrap it tightly in plastic wrap to keep it all together.
5. And now to eat. You can, of course, just take a bite from one end and keep going. Or you can be fancy and cut it on a diagonal before devouring. Enjoy!

Vegetables and Grains on the Side

Oven-Roasted Vegetables GF EF DF

Think of this more as a suggestion than an actual recipe—go ahead and mess with it to use whatever vegetables you happen to have in the house. Substitute chunks of butternut squash for sweet potatoes, or add some broccoli, cauliflower or carrots to the mix. Just make sure you cut everything up into similar-size pieces so they cook evenly.

2	medium sweet potatoes, peeled
2	medium onions
1	medium sweet red pepper
½ lb (250 g)	fresh mushrooms
1	medium zucchini
¼ cup (50 ml)	olive oil
2 cloves	garlic, minced or pressed
½ tsp (2 ml)	salt
	Chopped fresh parsley or basil (or both) if you have it

Preheat the oven to 425°F (220°C).

Trim all the vegetables, removing stems or cores or whatever the veggies happen to have, and cut into 1-inch (2 cm) chunks. If the mushrooms are very large, cut them in half; otherwise, leave them whole. Place in a bowl and toss with the olive oil, garlic and salt.

Spread vegetables out in single layer in a large, shallow baking pan—like a big lasagna pan. They need room to brown properly. Bake in the preheated oven for 40 to 45 minutes, tossing occasionally, until all the vegetables are tender and well browned.

Makes about 4 servings.

Ratatouille GF EF DF

Okay, we've all seen the movie. And we all know by now that there are no actual rats in ratatouille. It's a classic French vegetable concoction and you'll love it. Don't let the eggplant scare you off.

2 tbsp (30 ml)	olive or vegetable oil
4 cloves	garlic, minced or pressed
1	medium onion, chopped
2	medium zucchini, cut into ½-inch (1 cm) cubes
2	medium green or red peppers, diced
1	medium eggplant, cut into ½-inch (1 cm) cubes
¼ cup (50 ml)	chopped fresh basil (or 1 tbsp/15 ml dried)
2 cups (500 ml)	diced canned tomatoes (or about 4 medium fresh tomatoes, chopped)
1 tsp (2 ml)	salt
¼ tsp (1 ml)	pepper

Heat the olive oil in a very large skillet or Dutch oven over medium heat. Add the garlic and onion and cook until softened—about 5 minutes. Add the zucchini, peppers, eggplant and basil. Mix well, and cook, stirring, for about 10 minutes, or until the vegetables are almost tender (test with a fork to see). Add the tomatoes, salt and pepper, and cook for about 15 minutes more, stirring occasionally, until the vegetables are tender and the flavors are blended.

Serve hot or at room temperature.

Makes 6 to 8 servings as a side dish.

Lumpy Mashed Potatoes GF EF

You'll definitely want this with your meat loaf (for which, see page 80).

6	medium potatoes, peeled and cubed
½ cup (125 ml)	milk
¼ cup (50 ml)	butter
½ tsp (2 ml)	salt (or to taste)

First, you'll have to cook the potatoes. You can steam them or boil them. To steam, place your cubed potatoes in a steamer basket in a medium or large saucepan with ½ to 1 inch (1 to 2 cm) of water in the bottom. Cover, and cook over medium-high heat until the potatoes are completely tender when you poke a fork into them (the fork will go in with no resistance at all). To boil the potatoes, place them in a medium or large saucepan and add just enough water to cover them completely. Cover the pot, bring to a boil over medium-high heat and cook until tender (see fork test above).

While the potatoes are cooking, combine the milk and butter in a microwave-safe bowl or measuring cup, and microwave on high power for 1 to 1½ minutes. The milk should be hot and the butter melted. (If you don't have a microwave, heat the milk and butter together on the stove over medium heat—the milk doesn't have to boil.)

When the potatoes are done, drain off all the water, but leave the potatoes in the pot. Add the hot milk mixture and the salt, and mash with a potato masher or fork until the potatoes are light and fluffy, but just lumpy enough to prove you made them from scratch. (Never use a food processor or mixer to mash potatoes, because the potatoes can easily become gluey—and you *definitely* don't want gluey.)

Serve immediately if possible, or cover the dish and keep in a warm oven until you are ready.

Makes about 4 servings.

Oven-Fried Couch Potato Potatoes GF EF DF

There are times when crunchy hot potatoes are just the thing. These are delicious, addictive and a zillion times better than frozen French fries.

6	medium potatoes, washed and cut lengthwise into wedges (peel them if you feel you must)
¼ cup (50 ml)	olive oil or vegetable oil
1 tbsp (15 ml)	lemon juice
½ tsp (2 ml)	salt
¼ tsp (1 ml)	black pepper

Preheat the oven to 450°F (230°C). Grease a 9 x 13-inch (23 x 33 cm) baking dish.

Dump the potatoes into the prepared baking dish, drizzle them with the oil and lemon juice, and sprinkle with salt and pepper to taste. Toss to coat everything evenly and then spread the potato wedges out in the pan so that they're in a single layer.

Place in the oven and bake for at least 45 minutes, stirring them from time to time, until they're crisp and golden on all sides and perfectly tender inside.

Serve immediately with the usual French fry accompaniments.

Now, isn't that better than anything?

Makes as many as 4 servings as a side dish, but only a measly 2 servings as a stand-alone snack.

Go crazy

Don't be afraid to try sprinkling the potatoes with seasoned salt, cayenne pepper, paprika, fresh or granulated garlic or crumbled herbs. Add this stuff with the salt and pepper before the pan goes in the oven.

Scalloped Potatoes EF

Here's a side dish that really wants to be the main course. Give it a chance at stardom! The baking time is longish, so plan for this.

2 tbsp (30 ml)	all-purpose flour
1 tsp (5 ml)	salt
¼ tsp (1 ml)	pepper
6 to 8	medium potatoes, peeled and sliced very thin (8 cups/2 l sliced)
1½ cups (375 ml)	grated cheddar or Swiss cheese
2 tbsp (30 ml)	butter
2½ cups (625 ml)	milk

Preheat the oven to 375°F (190°C). Grease a 9 x 13-inch (23 x 33 cm) baking dish.

In a small bowl, mix the flour, salt and pepper.

Arrange about a third of the potato slices over the bottom of the prepared baking dish. Sprinkle evenly with about half the flour mixture and cover with half the grated cheese. Repeat with a second layer of potatoes (half of what you have left) and all the rest of the flour mixture and cheese. Finally, cover with the remaining potato slices, dot the top with butter and pour the milk over everything. Cover the baking dish with foil, place in the preheated oven and bake for 45 minutes. Remove the foil and continue baking for another 45 to 50 minutes, or until the top is browned and the potatoes are completely tender when you poke a knife into the middle of the dish.

Makes 6 to 8 servings.

Refried Beans GF EF DF

Canned refried beans can be salty, greasy and really not that great. Some brands contain lard—a problem if you're a vegetarian; some may include artificial preservatives or other things you'd prefer to avoid. Make your own—they're easy, cheap and you know exactly what goes into them.

2 tbsp (30 ml)	olive oil or vegetable oil
½ cup (125 ml)	finely chopped onion
1 clove	garlic, squished
1 can (19 oz/540 ml)	kidney, pinto, romano or black beans
½ tsp (2 ml)	salt if needed

In a medium skillet, heat the oil over medium heat. Add the onion and garlic, and sauté, stirring occasionally, for about 5 minutes, or until soft. Add the canned beans, including their liquid, to the pan and cook, mashing with a wooden spoon or a potato masher, until the mixture is fairly thick and about half mashed. You can add a bit more liquid (water or broth) if you think the beans are getting too dry. Taste, and add salt if needed.

Makes about 2 cups (500 ml) refried beans, to use in whatever way your little heart desires. See below for suggestions.

What to Do with Refried Beans

- Fill burritos (see page 157)
- Layer with salsa and guacamole as a dip for tortilla chips
- Make Fully Loaded Nachos (see page 196)
- Serve with scrambled eggs and salsa for a Mexican breakfast
- Spread on a wrap (see page 52)

How to Cook Frozen Vegetables

Frozen vegetables are great to have around. They're cheap, they don't go rotten and they taste fresher than canned. Some actually taste better and retain more nutrients than the "fresh" ones that have spent a week or two hitchhiking from Mexico to your supermarket. And in deepest, darkest February, when even the crummiest cabbage costs a month's rent, you'll want to put something green on your plate, won't you?

The best of the frozen bunch are peas, corn, green and yellow beans, broccoli, and cauliflower. Some of the frozen-vegetable medleys are neat if you just want a pile of different things to throw in a soup or stir-fry.

Buying frozen carrots is silly because fresh ones are always good and cheap. Frozen asparagus and zucchini are disappointingly soggy and frozen potatoes are just plain weird. Also avoid veggies frozen in sauce—they're often expensive, and high in salt and other things you don't need.

Whenever possible, buy the kind of frozen vegetables sold loose in bags. That way you can use just the amount you need, reseal the bag and toss it back into the freezer.

Regular Cooking

Bring a pot of water to a boil. Add the vegetables, let the water to return to a boil and cook for 2 to 8 minutes, depending on the vegetable.

Steam cooking

Place frozen vegetables in a steamer basket or colander over boiling water and steam for 2 to 8 minutes, until they're done the way you like them.

Microwave cooking

Put frozen vegetables in a microwave-safe dish, add 1 tbsp (15 ml) of water for each cup of vegetables and cover with a lid or plastic wrap. Microwave on high power for 3 to 5 minutes, stirring a couple of times.

An Incomplete Guide to Vegetable Cookery

So there it sits. Broccoli. Or spinach. Or whatever it is. You've eaten it cooked, but how do you get there? This thing is *raw!* Relax—it's just a harmless vegetable. You're bigger and smarter and you have a knife. Here are some guidelines to help you grapple with the most common vegetables you'll likely encounter.

Carrots

Scrub well and peel if you want. Cut into slices or dice into cubes. Steam in a steamer basket over boiling water, or boil in water or broth until tender but still a bit firm. Fresh carrots are also surprisingly delicious sautéed in butter or olive oil.

Green or yellow beans

Wash and snap off the stem end. Don't worry about the other, pointy, end—it's edible. Cut beans into pieces or leave whole. Steam in a steamer basket over boiling water, or boil in water until the color brightens and the beans become tender but are still a little crisp.

Broccoli

Wash well and cut off the bottom of each stem. Cut the stem crosswise into chunks and separate the top into bite-size florets. Steam in a steamer basket over boiling water, or boil in water until the broccoli becomes bright green. At this point the broccoli is perfect—tender but still crisp. Overcooked broccoli is mushy and swampy green, and loses all its charm.

Cauliflower

A relative of broccoli, cauliflower can be prepared the same way (see above). For a real treat, try roasting it. If you think you don't like cauliflower, this may change your mind. With a sharp knife, cut the cauliflower into bite-size florets and place in a bowl. Drizzle with olive oil and toss until all the pieces are lightly coated, then sprinkle with a little salt and pepper. Dump onto a cookie sheet or shallow baking pan and spread the pieces in a single layer. Roast at 425°F (220°C) for 30 to 40 minutes, stirring once or twice, until lightly browned. Shockingly good.

Zucchini

Wash and slice crosswise into ¼-inch (.5 cm) pieces. Or cut into ½-inch (1 cm) cubes. Your choice. Zucchini is best sautéed in a little olive or vegetable oil over medium-high heat. It plays well with onions, peppers and garlic.

Spinach

Pick over the spinach and remove any wilted leaves or odd bits of some other plant. Rinse well (even if the package says already washed) and drain. For simple steamed spinach, cram the wet leaves into a pot, cover with a lid and let cook over medium-high heat until wilted. You won't need any more water than what was already clinging to the leaves. Drain off the excess liquid and you're done. You can also tear up the raw spinach leaves and add them to a stir-fry or soup.

Winter Squash

This confusing group includes butternut squash, hubbard squash, acorn or pepper squash, even pumpkins—to name just a few. You can simply cut most squash in half, scrape out the seeds and bake. Place the squash halves, cut-side down, on a cookie sheet or shallow baking pan with a small amount of water in the bottom of the pan. Bake at 400°F (200°C) for about 45 minutes (longer or shorter, depending on the squash). Halfway through the baking time, turn the squash over— cut-side up—and add a blob of butter to the cavity. The squash is done if it's tender when you poke a fork into the thickest part. Scoop out the flesh and mash, or serve the baked squash halves just the way they are.

Mushrooms

Regular white or light brown (cremini) mushrooms should be rinsed to remove any dirt, then drained well. Trim the dried end off the stems and slice or cut the mushrooms in half. They're best sautéed in butter or olive oil and play well with onions and garlic. You can prepare portobello mushrooms the same way, or you can cut them into large chunks, brush them with oil and roast (see cauliflower).

Asparagus

Sorry—did that scare you? No really—asparagus is easy. Rinse and trim off the cut end of each spear. Steam (see broccoli) until bright green and not a moment longer. Or roast (see cauliflower) for 15 to 20 minutes, until beginning to brown. Either way you'll love it.

Corn

On the cob, of course. Peel off the husk, pull off the hairy bits and either steam the cob in a steamer basket over boiling water or boil in water for at least 5 minutes but no more than 10. The kernels should be tender but still have some crunch when you take a bite.

How to Cook Rice

You don't ever need to use instant rice. The real thing tastes better, is cheaper and doesn't take very much time to make anyway. The ratio of rice to liquid can vary depending on the type of rice you have. If your rice turns out too mushy, use less liquid next time. If it's not quite cooked, add a bit more liquid.

White Rice

Simple, basic and it goes with anything.

   1 cup (250 ml)   white rice (see page 69 for different varieties)
1½ cups (375 ml)   water

Measure the water into a saucepan with a tight-fitting lid. Bring it to a boil over high heat. Add the rice to the boiling water and give it a stir. Lower the heat to the barest simmer and cover with the lid. Let cook for 15 minutes without peeking.

After 15 minutes, lift the lid and have a look. The water should be completely absorbed and the surface of the rice should look as if there are holes all over it. Don't stir, but taste a grain or two to see if the rice is done. If it's not quite cooked, replace the lid and give it another 5 minutes, then taste a grain again. When the rice is cooked, remove the pan from the heat and let stand, covered, for about 5 minutes, then fluff with a fork and serve.

Makes about 3 cups (625 ml) of plain white rice.

Brown Rice

Slightly chewy, nutty, delicious. Brown rice takes a little longer to cook than white, but it's terribly good for you and it goes well with beans and other hearty things.

   1 cup (250 ml)   brown rice (see page 69 for different varieties)
2¼ cups (625 ml)   water

Measure the water into a saucepan with a tight-fitting lid. Bring it to a boil over high heat. Add the rice to the boiling water and give it a stir.

Lower the heat to the barest simmer and cover with the lid. Let cook for 35 minutes without peeking.

After 35 minutes, lift the lid and have a look. The water should be completely absorbed and the surface of the rice should look as if there are holes all over it. Don't stir, but taste a grain or two to see if the rice is cooked. If it's not quite cooked, replace the lid and give it another 5 minutes, then taste it again. When the rice is cooked, remove the pan from the heat and let stand, covered, for about 5 minutes, then fluff with a fork and serve.

Makes 3½ cups (875 ml) plain brown rice.

Lemon Rice GF EF

Serve this flavorful lemony rice as a side dish with chicken or fish.

2 tbsp (30 ml)	butter
1 cup (250 ml)	long grain white rice (basmati is great if you have it)
½ tsp (2 ml)	salt
½ tsp (2 ml)	turmeric
1	lemon, zest grated and juice squeezed
	Water (see below)

In a saucepan with a tightly fitting lid, melt the butter over medium heat. Add the rice, salt, turmeric and lemon zest, and sauté, stirring constantly, for 2 or 3 minutes—just until the rice begins to look shiny.

Pour the lemon juice into a measuring cup and add enough water to make a total of 2 cups (500 ml) liquid. Add this to the rice mixture in the saucepan and bring to a boil. Cover the pan, reduce the heat to low and cook, without peeking, for 20 minutes, or until all the liquid has been absorbed and holes begin to appear on the surface of the rice (yes, peek now). Remove from heat, let sit for 5 minutes, then fluff with a fork and serve.

Makes about 3 cups (750 ml).

Indian-ish Rice Pilaf with Vegetables GF EF DF

This can be a side dish or a main dish. It's full of vegetables, exotically spiced (but not hot) and goes just as well with curry as it does with a saucy meat concoction or a good old burger. You can use 2 cups (500 ml) frozen mixed vegetables instead of the peas, carrot, pepper and zucchini if you can't be bothered to do all that chopping.

2 tbsp (30 ml)	butter, olive oil or vegetable oil
1	small onion, chopped
1 tsp (5 ml)	curry powder
¼ tsp (1 ml)	cinnamon
1 clove	garlic, minced or pressed
½ cup (125 ml)	frozen peas
½ cup (125 ml)	diced carrot
½ cup (125 ml)	chopped green or red sweet pepper
½ cup (125 ml)	diced zucchini
1 cup (250 ml)	long grain white or brown rice (basmati, if you have it)
2 cups (500 ml)	water
½ tsp (2 ml)	salt
½ cup (125 ml)	raisins

Heat the butter or oil in a large pot over medium heat, add the onion and cook, stirring occasionally, for 5 to 7 minutes, or until beginning to turn golden. Add the curry powder, cinnamon and garlic, stir, then add all the vegetables and the rice. Cook over medium heat, stirring often, for about 5 minutes. Now add the water, salt and raisins, and bring to a boil. Turn the heat down very low, cover the pot with a tight-fitting lid and cook for about 20 to 25 minutes, until all the water is absorbed. Remove from heat and let stand, covered, for about 5 minutes, then fluff with a fork and serve.

Makes about 4 servings.

Carnivore alert

Turn this vegetarian pilaf into a non-vegetarian main dish by adding 2 cups (500 ml) diced cooked chicken, beef, pork or shrimp to the finished dish. Just toss it into the rice mixture about 5 minutes before the pilaf is done cooking to allow the addition to heat through.

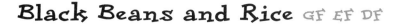

Black Beans and Rice GF EF DF

Beans and rice go together like, um, shoes and socks. Only, they taste much better. Serve this as a side dish with something meaty, or add a salad and it's a main dish all on its own. You can even wrap beans and rice into a tortilla with a spoonful of salsa, some lettuce and shredded cheese for a delicious burrito. Who wouldn't love something like this?

6 slices	bacon, cut into 1-inch (2 cm) pieces
1	onion, chopped
2 cloves	garlic, minced or pressed
2 cups (500 ml)	beef, chicken or vegetable broth (prepared broth or made from bouillon cubes or powder)
1 cup (250 ml)	white rice
1 cup (250 ml)	diced tomatoes (canned are fine)
½	medium green pepper, diced
1 tsp (5 ml)	thyme
1 tsp (5 ml)	cumin
1 can (19 oz/540 ml)	black beans, drained and rinsed
1 tbsp (15 ml)	chopped fresh cilantro or parsley (optional)

Cook the bacon in a medium saucepan over medium heat until just beginning to get crisp—about 5 to 7 minutes. With a slotted spoon, remove the bacon pieces to a plate and drain off almost all the fat, leaving just about 1 tbsp (15 ml) in the saucepan. Add the onion and garlic to the pot, and cook for about 5 minutes, stirring frequently, until softened.

Pour the beef broth into the pan and bring it to a boil, stirring to dissolve the brown bits on the bottom of the pan. Stir in the rice, tomatoes, green pepper, thyme, cumin and bacon pieces, and mix well. Cover tightly, reduce the heat to low and simmer for 15 minutes. Stir in the beans and cook for another 5 minutes, just until heated through. Sprinkle with chopped cilantro or parsley (if you're using it) before serving.

Makes about 4 to 6 servings as a side dish or main.

Vegetarian alert

Omit the bacon and sauté the onions and garlic in 1 tbsp (15 ml) olive or vegetable oil, use vegetable broth as the cooking liquid and ta-da! Vegetarian black beans and rice!

Crazy Easy Mushroom Risotto GF EF

Maybe you've eaten risotto in a restaurant or at someone's home. This Italian rice dish is often considered time-consuming to make (it isn't) and finicky (not at all). Try this simplified recipe and you may just impress your Italian grandmother. If you have one, that is.

2 tbsp (30 ml)	olive oil or vegetable oil
1 tbsp (15 ml)	butter
1	medium onion, chopped
8 oz (250 g)	mushrooms, thinly sliced (3 cups/750 ml)
1½ cups (375 ml)	arborio rice (yes, you should use it)
4 cups (1 l)	chicken or vegetable broth (prepared broth or made from bouillon cubes or powder)
¼ cup (50 ml)	grated Parmesan cheese (and a bit more to sprinkle at the table)
	Salt and pepper to taste

Combine the oil and butter in a medium saucepan that has a lid and place it over medium heat. Add the onion and cook, stirring often, until soft and beginning to turn golden—about 7 minutes. Add the mushrooms, increase the heat to medium high and cook, stirring, until the mushrooms have softened, released their juices and the liquid has almost completely evaporated—5 to 7 minutes. Now add the rice and stir for a couple of minutes, then add all the broth. Bring to a boil, stirring to prevent the rice from sticking to the bottom of the pot. Reduce the heat to low, cover the pot with the lid and cook—without stirring or looking or any kind of fussing whatsoever—for 15 minutes.

After 15 minutes, remove the lid, stir in the Parmesan cheese and season to taste with salt and pepper. The risotto should be creamy but not runny. If it's too dry, you can add a bit of water or broth. The risotto will thicken as it cools.

Serve immediately with additional Parmesan for sprinkling at the table.

Makes 4 servings.

Risotto possibilities

Don't like mushrooms? No problem. Just leave them out—the dish will still be good.

Other veggies will work too. Try chopped asparagus, broccoli, peas or spinach instead of mushrooms. Stir in 2 or 3 cups (500 to 750 ml) of any of these vegetables when you add the broth—don't sauté them with the onions because the veggies will overcook.

Serve risotto as a side dish with something stewy, or as a main dish with a crisp green salad. *Fantastico!*

Not-So-Plain Grains

Once in a while a person needs something else. Not rice, but sort of like rice. Something to soak up the sauce or serve with the stew. Here are a couple of nifty alternatives when you're feeling a little wild and crazy.

Quinoa

Pronounced *keen-wah*, this cute little grain was a favorite with the Incas of Peru. It's extremely nutritious, really tasty and very easy to cook. You can serve it as a side dish—it's like rice, only more fun. (Look closely at the cooked grains—they're adorable!)

1 cup (250 ml)	quinoa
1½ cups (375 ml)	water

Before cooking quinoa, you need to rinse it. Measure it into a strainer (with small holes) and run water over it, stirring it with your fingers to make sure it's well rinsed. Let it drain while you bring the water to a boil. (Some packaged quinoa is prerinsed, making this step unnecessary—it will say so on the package. If you're not sure, just rinse before using.)

Measure the water into a saucepan with a tight-fitting lid. Bring water to a boil over high heat. Add the rinsed quinoa and give it a stir. When the water returns to a boil, turn the heat down to low, cover the pot and let it cook, undisturbed, for 15 minutes. Turn off the heat and let the quinoa sit for another 5 minutes before serving. That's it.

Makes 2½ cups (625 ml) cooked quinoa.

Couscous

Technically, couscous is a tiny form of pasta. It's made from wheat and comes in different varieties—regular, whole wheat, vegetable flavored. It cooks in minutes and goes with just about anything. What's not to like?

1 cup (250 ml)	water or broth
1 tbsp (15 ml)	olive oil, vegetable oil or butter
1 cup (250 ml)	couscous
½ tsp (2 ml)	salt

In a medium saucepan, combine the liquid with the oil or butter and bring to a boil over high heat. Stir in the dry couscous and salt, cover and remove from heat. Let stand for 5 to 10 minutes. The grains will have absorbed all the liquid and become tender. Fluff with a fork and serve.

No, seriously—that's it.

Makes about 2 cups (500 ml) couscous

Couscous gone wild

Herbed Lemon Couscous—stir in 1 tbsp (15 ml) chopped fresh parsley and 1 tbsp (15 ml) lemon juice when you add the couscous to the liquid.

Rock the Casbah Couscous—stir in 2 tbsp (30 ml) raisins, ¼ tsp (1 ml) cinnamon, ¼ tsp (1 ml) turmeric and ¼ tsp (1 ml) ground cumin when you add the couscous to the liquid.

Tomato Basil Couscous—add 2 chopped sun-dried tomatoes, 2 chopped green onions and 1 tbsp (15 ml) chopped fresh basil when you stir the couscous into the liquid.

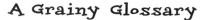

A Grainy Glossary

Arborio rice
Italian short grain rice, essential for risotto and very good for rice pudding.

Barley
A delicious chewy grain that's great in soup and salad, and good as a side dish in place of rice

Basmati rice—white and brown
Aromatic rice from India with a wonderfully nutty flavor— very fluffy, with long grains.

Brown rice
What white rice was before they sanded the outsides off. Tasty, chewy, full of vitamins, fiber and other good stuff.

Buckwheat (kasha)
An earthy-tasting grain, available either toasted or untoasted and great with mushrooms and onions.

Bulgur wheat
Cracked wheat that has been completely cooked and then dehydrated. Makes a great pilaf, and essential for tabouli salad.

Converted rice
Steamed before milling. The grains stay separate when cooked and the rice retains more vitamins than regular white rice.

Couscous
Actually a teensy pasta, not a grain. Made from wheat, it cooks in minutes.

Instant rice
Rice that has been completely cooked, then dehydrated. Useful for mountain climbing and other desperate survival situations.

Jasmine rice
A fragrant, medium grain rice. Widely used in Thai and other Asian cooking.

Long grain white rice
All-purpose rice that cooks up fluffy and white. Easily available everywhere.

Quinoa
A rediscovered ancient Inca grain. Extremely nutritious— high in protein and minerals.

Short grain white rice
Stickier than long grain and a little chewy. Especially good for Asian dishes.

Wild rice
Technically not rice at all, but it looks sort of like it. Very tasty, brown and chewy, and often quite expensive.

Mainly Meat

A Perfect Hamburger GF EF DF

Perfection, hamburgerwise, is in the taste buds of the beholder. Some people like to add a lot of stuff to their burger mixture; others like to put lots of stuff on top after cooking. Here's a basic recipe that you can mess with until you've found *your* burger nirvana.

1 lb (500 g)	lean ground beef
¼ cup (50 ml)	water (yes, water—it keeps them moist)
½ tsp (2 ml)	salt
¼ tsp (1 ml)	pepper

In a bowl, with a fork or bare-handed, mix the ground beef with the water, salt and pepper. Gently. The secret to a perfect burger is not to handle the meat too much—so don't mush it to death.

With a light touch, form it into 3 or 4 patties, squishing them just enough so they don't fall apart. Flatten the burgers to an even thickness—around ½ inch (1 cm) is good. (Your burgers will shrink as they cook.) Place on a plate—cover and refrigerate until you're ready to cook them.

If you're using a barbecue grill or oven broiler, preheat it to medium high. If you're cooking your burgers on a skillet, place it over medium-high heat with 1 tbsp (15 ml) vegetable oil.

Whichever method you're using, cook your burgers until they're evenly browned on both sides, flipping them once or twice, until they're no longer pink in the middle (cut into one to check). If your heat is too high, the outsides of the burgers may burn before the insides are done—reduce the heat so they cook through without becoming incinerated.

Serve on a lightly toasted bun, with absolutely everything on it. Especially hot peppers.

Makes 3 large or 4 regular burgers. *Perfect* ones.

Burgers gone wild

To the basic recipe, you can add any of the following ingredients (but not all at once!). Purists may disapprove, but what you do to your burger is nobody's business.

¼ cup (50 ml)	bread crumbs
¼ cup (50 ml)	finely chopped onion
1 clove	garlic, minced
¼ cup (50 ml)	barbecue sauce, ketchup or salsa
2 tbsp (30 ml)	grated Parmesan cheese
1 tbsp (15 ml)	finely chopped parsley or green onion
1 tbsp (15 ml)	Worcestershire sauce
1 tsp (5 ml)	hot pepper sauce

Stuffed Peppers DF

Stuffing peppers is a very satisfying thing to do. They don't require any fancy folding, they're sturdy enough to withstand a certain amount of abuse and they bounce rather nicely if you happen to drop one on the floor (not on purpose).

1 lb (500 g)	lean ground beef or turkey
½ cup (125 ml)	uncooked white rice
1	small onion, chopped
1	egg
1 tsp (5 ml)	salt
¼ tsp (1 ml)	black pepper
6 to 8	small to medium green (or any color) sweet peppers
2 tbsp (30 ml)	olive oil or vegetable oil
2 tbsp (30 ml)	all-purpose flour
6 cups (1.5 l)	tomato juice (one 48 oz/1.36 liter can or bottle)
1 tbsp (15 ml)	granulated sugar
	Additional salt and pepper to taste

Preheat the oven to 350°F (180°C).

In a medium bowl, combine the ground beef or turkey, rice, onion, egg, salt and pepper. Stir with a fork or mush with your (clean) bare hands until well mixed.

Prepare the green peppers by cutting around the stem end of each pepper and pulling out the stem and seed clump. Stuff the peppers lightly with the meat mixture, filling them about ¾ full (the stuffing will expand as it cooks). This amount of stuffing should fill 6 to 8 peppers, depending on the size. (If you run out of peppers before you run out of stuffing, just form the meat into little balls and toss them into the sauce to cook.)

In a very large ovenproof pot or Dutch oven with a cover, combine the oil with the flour and cook gently over low heat for 1 or 2 minutes, stirring constantly. Add the tomato juice gradually, stirring to avoid lumps, increase the heat to medium and bring to a boil. The sauce will thicken slightly. Stir in the sugar, and add salt and pepper if you think they're needed.

Carefully place the stuffed peppers in the tomato sauce, arranging them so that they're standing in the pot. The sauce should just about cover the peppers, but if it doesn't, spoon some on top of the meat filling to keep it moistened. Bring the pot of peppers to a boil, cover with a lid and place in the preheated oven. Bake for 1½ hours,

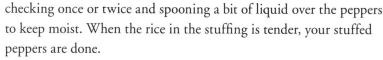

checking once or twice and spooning a bit of liquid over the peppers to keep moist. When the rice in the stuffing is tender, your stuffed peppers are done.

Serve stuffed peppers generously drowned in the tomato sauce. Makes 4 to 6 servings.

Practice Safe Beef

Ground beef—the gateway meat for most beginning cooks—is so easy to cook that you may take it for granted as utterly goofproof. Unfortunately, beneath that innocent exterior lurks a minefield of potential hazards. Learn how to safely handle and cook ground beef to avoid icky consequences.

- Buy meat that has been properly refrigerated (or frozen) and keep it cold until you begin cooking.
- At the store, double-bag ground beef (or any meat, for that matter) so that the juices don't leak out onto your other groceries. Those juices are a bacterial breeding ground and can contaminate other foods if you're not careful.
- Thaw frozen ground beef slowly in the refrigerator or quickly in the microwave on the defrost setting. Don't leave it at room temperature for more than an hour—bacteria just love a nice romantic hunk of hamburger in which to multiply.
- Cook hamburgers (and other ground beef concoctions) until the meat is no longer pink inside—on a meat thermometer this would be 160°F (71°C). At that temperature, any bacteria lurking in the meat will have been destroyed, making the food safe to eat.
- Refrigerate leftovers as soon as possible after cooking—don't let the meat linger in the danger zone (not hot, not cold) for any longer than absolutely necessary.

Plain Old Meatballs EF

These are basic meatballs searching for fulfillment. Should they settle for spaghetti? Or should they wait for something more exotic and go Hawaiian? Or would they be wise to just go it alone on a toothpick? Only you can decide.

1 lb (500 g)	lean ground beef (or turkey)
1	egg
½ cup (125 ml)	bread crumbs
¼ cup (50 ml)	*very* finely chopped onion
1 tsp (5 ml)	salt
½ tsp (2 ml)	pepper

Preheat the oven to 375°F (190°C). Lightly grease a cookie sheet.

In a medium bowl, combine the ground beef, egg, bread crumbs, onion, salt and pepper. Smush together with a fork or clean bare hands until well mixed. Form into 1-inch (2 cm) meatballs, rolling them between your hands so they're nice and round. Place meatballs in one layer on the prepared cookie sheet and bake for 15 to 20 minutes, turning them over halfway through baking, or until lightly browned and cooked through.

Scoop the meatballs off the cookie sheet, leaving any fat that has drained out of them behind. Use in any recipe that calls for Plain Old Meatballs—such as Hawaiian Meatballs (page 75), Killer Barbecue Meatballs (page 76) or Classic Spaghetti with Meatballs (page 120).

Makes enough meatballs for 4 servings, more or less.

Hawaiian Meatballs EF

If it has pineapple in it, it must be from Hawaii, right? Well, maybe. Whatever—it's good.

1 batch	Plain Old Meatballs (recipe on page 74), browned
1 can (14 oz/398 ml)	pineapple chunks
¼ cup (50 ml)	brown sugar
3 tbsp (45 ml)	vinegar
2 tbsp (30 ml)	cornstarch
2 tbsp (30 ml)	soy sauce
½ tsp (2 ml)	ground ginger
1	green pepper, cut into large squares
1	onion, cut into large squares

Drain the pineapple chunks and pour the juice into a measuring cup. Add enough water to the juice to make 1¼ cups (300 ml) of liquid. Pour this into a large saucepan or Dutch oven. (Try to restrain yourself from eating all the pineapple chunks—you'll be needing them later.)

To the juice in the saucepan, stir in the brown sugar, vinegar, cornstarch, soy sauce and ginger. Place over medium heat and bring the mixture to a simmer, stirring constantly, until the sauce is clear and thickened. Dump in the entire batch of Plain Old Meatballs, cooked and drained, and simmer them in the sauce for 5 minutes, stirring once or twice. Add the green pepper, onion and pineapple chunks, and continue to cook for 5 to 10 minutes, or until the vegetables are tender but still crisp.

Serve immediately with white or brown rice.

Makes 4 servings.

Killer Barbecue Meatballs EF

Are you brave enough to face these lethal meatballs? Of course you are.

1 batch	Plain Old Meatballs (recipe on page 74), browned
2 cups (500 ml)	canned crushed tomatoes
1 cup (250 ml)	ketchup
½ cup (125 ml)	cider or white vinegar
½ cup (125 ml)	brown sugar
½	medium onion, chopped
4 cloves	garlic, minced or pressed
1 tbsp (15 ml)	Worcestershire sauce
1 tbsp (15 ml)	Mexican chili powder
1 tbsp (15 ml)	prepared mustard (Dijon, if you have it)
½ tsp (2 ml)	cayenne pepper (more cayenne if you like—they're your meatballs)

In a medium saucepan, combine the crushed tomatoes, ketchup, vinegar, sugar, onion, garlic, Worcestershire, chili powder, mustard and cayenne. Place over medium heat and cook, stirring, for about 10 minutes. Taste, and adjust the seasoning to your level of bravery. Plunk in the browned meatballs and continue to simmer, covered, for about 15 to 20 minutes, stirring occasionally.

Serve meatballs over rice, with potatoes or as an appetizer on toothpicks.

Makes about 4 servings as a main dish.

The Ultimate Sloppy Joe GF EF DF

Messy, runny, meaty, delicious. Go no further—you've arrived at Sloppy Joe perfection.

2 tbsp (30 ml)	olive oil or vegetable oil
1	medium onion, chopped
1 stalk	celery, chopped
1 cup (250 ml)	coarsely chopped mushrooms
1 lb (500 g)	lean ground beef or ground turkey
¼ cup (50 ml)	beef broth (prepared broth or made from bouillon cube or powder)
¼ cup (50 ml)	ketchup
½ tsp (2 ml)	salt
½ tsp (2 ml)	hot pepper sauce (or more or less or none)
	Black pepper to taste

Heat the oil in a large skillet, add the onion, celery and mushrooms, then cook over medium heat until soft—7 to 10 minutes. Crumble in the ground beef or turkey and cook, stirring to break up the lumps, until the meat is no longer pink—5 to 7 minutes. Add the broth, ketchup and hot pepper sauce, and simmer for another 5 minutes, or until everything is nicely glopped together.

Spoon over 4 toasted hamburger buns and eat—sloppily.

Ramen Noodle Dinner EF DF

Absolutely idiotically easy, this is the fastest emergency dinner there is. Fifteen minutes, start to finish.

1 tsp (5 ml)	vegetable oil
1 lb (500 g)	lean ground beef
1 pkg	ramen noodle soup, any flavor
2 cups (500 ml)	fresh bean sprouts, rinsed
4	green onions, trimmed and sliced
1 can (14.5 oz/428 ml)	stewed tomatoes (about 2 cups/500 ml)

In a large skillet, heat the vegetable oil over medium heat. Add the ground beef and cook, stirring to break up the lumps, until no longer pink. Drain off any fat (not down the sink, please).

Sprinkle in the flavor packet from the noodles, then add the bean sprouts, green onions and tomatoes. Bring to a boil. Crumble in the noodles, cover the pan and cook for 8 to 10 minutes, or until the noodles are tender and the whole mess is done. That's it.

Serves 3 or 4.

Totally Excellent Chili GF EF DF

To be totally excellent, chili must be spicy (but not necessarily hot) and runny enough to eat with a spoon (but not soupy). Leave out or reduce the amount of hot pepper or cayenne if you prefer a mild chili—this dish will still have plenty of flavor.

1½ lbs (750 g)	lean ground beef
2	large onions, chopped
2 cloves	garlic, minced or pressed
1 can (28 oz/796 ml)	diced tomatoes
1 tbsp (15 ml)	Mexican chili powder
2 tsp (10 ml)	ground cumin
1½ tsp (7 ml)	salt
½ tsp (2 ml)	curry powder
½ tsp (2 ml)	cayenne pepper (or one small fresh jalapeño, minced—or both)
2 cans (19 oz/540 ml each)	red kidney or pinto beans, drained and rinsed

In a large saucepan or Dutch oven, combine the ground beef with the onions and garlic, and cook, stirring to break up the clumps, until the meat is no longer pink. Add the tomatoes, chili powder, cumin, salt, curry powder and cayenne or jalapeño, and simmer for about 30 minutes, stirring frequently. Add the beans and cook for another 30 minutes.

Serve this Totally Excellent Chili with plain rice or freshly baked corn bread (see page 161), sprinkled with shredded cheese. If the chili is too hot, a spoonful of plain yogurt or sour cream will help cool things down.

Makes about 6 servings.

Twenty-Minute Tacos EF

It's midnight. You need tacos. Can you wait 20 minutes?

1 lb (500 ml)	lean ground beef, chicken or turkey
½	medium onion, chopped
½	medium green pepper, chopped
1 clove	garlic, minced or pressed
1 cup (250 ml)	tomato sauce (any kind—even leftover spaghetti sauce is fine)
1 tbsp (15 ml)	Mexican chili powder
½ tsp (2 ml)	salt
¼ tsp (1 ml)	cayenne pepper (or more or less)
12-ish	6-inch/15 cm flour tortillas (for soft tacos) or crisp taco shells (for crunchy ones)
	Taco toppings: shredded lettuce, diced tomatoes, salsa, shredded cheese, sour cream, chopped onions, diced avocado, jalapeño peppers, chocolate chips (just kidding)

Preheat the oven to 300°F (160°C).

If you're using flour tortillas, wrap them tightly in foil and place in the oven to warm while you prepare the filling. If you're using crisp taco shells, arrange them on a baking pan and place in the oven to warm.

In a large skillet, combine the ground beef (or whatever), the onion, green pepper and garlic. Cook over medium heat, stirring to break up lumps, for 8 to 10 minutes, or until the meat is browned and the onions and green pepper are softened. Drain off any fat.

Add the tomato sauce, chili powder, cayenne and salt. Cook, stirring, over medium heat for 7 to 10 minutes, until the mixture is thick enough to spoon into a tortilla or taco shell without running out the sides.

Remove the tortillas or taco shells from the oven and spoon in some of the meat mixture. Add your choice of taco toppings and take a bite. Quick! Make another!

Makes about 12 tacos.

101 Mom's Dreaded Meat Loaf DF

Did your mom make this every Wednesday? Did you have to take meat loaf sandwiches to school? Did you hate them? Do you miss them now? Here—make this.

1½ lbs (750 g)	lean ground beef
1 cup (250 ml)	soft bread crumbs
2	eggs, beaten
1	small onion, finely chopped
1 cup (250 ml)	tomato juice
1 tsp (5 ml)	salt
½ tsp (2 ml)	black pepper
1 or 2	hard-boiled eggs, peeled (optional but fun)
¼ cup (50 ml)	ketchup

Preheat the oven to 350°F (180°C).

In a large bowl, combine the ground beef, bread crumbs, beaten eggs, onion, tomato juice, salt and pepper. Mix well, using your bare hands or a large fork, until everything is evenly combined. (Bare-handed mixing is a truly primal experience and highly recommended—but don't forget to wash your hands before and after.)

At this point, you have two choices: You can either squish the mixture into a 9 x 5-inch (23 x 13 cm) loaf pan to bake (simple, straightforward, very fast), or you can shape a loaf by hand and bake it loose in a 9 x 13-inch (23 x 33 cm) baking dish (this allows for more creative expression). Clearly, you'll want to make your meat loaf exactly the way your mom did.

What to do with the hard-boiled eggs? So glad you asked. Bury them in the center of your meat loaf as a sort of hidden treasure. Looks nice when the meat loaf is sliced, but not critical to the success of the actual loaf.

With a basting brush, paint the surface of the meat loaf with the ketchup and bake for 1 hour and 15 minutes, or until cooked right through. Let stand 5 to 10 minutes before slicing.

Eat with mashed potatoes and something green.

Makes 5 to 6 servings.

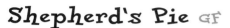

Shepherd's Pie GF

You don't have to be a shepherd to make this dish. Or to love it.

2 tbsp (30 ml)	olive oil or vegetable oil
1	onion, chopped
2 cloves	garlic, squished
1	medium sweet green or red pepper, diced
2 cups (500 ml)	sliced fresh mushrooms
1	carrot, diced
1½ lbs (750 g)	lean ground beef or turkey
1 cup (250 ml)	frozen peas
1 cup (250 ml)	ketchup, spaghetti sauce or salsa
4	large potatoes, peeled and cut into chunks
2 tbsp (30 ml)	butter
½ cup (125 ml)	milk
1 tsp (5 ml)	salt
¼ tsp (1 ml)	black pepper

Preheat the oven to 350°F (180°C).

Heat the oil in a large skillet over medium heat. Add the onion and garlic, and cook for about 5 minutes, or until softened. Add the peppers, mushrooms and carrots, and continue cooking for another 5 to 7 minutes, or until the carrots are almost tender. Add the ground beef or turkey to the skillet and cook, stirring to break up the clumps for another 6 to 8 minutes, or until the meat is no longer pink. Add the peas, stir in the ketchup (or whatever you're using), salt and pepper, and continue to cook for 10 minutes. Dump into an 8- or 9-inch (20 or 23 cm) square baking dish.

While the meat mixture is cooking, prepare the mashed potato topping. Cook the potatoes in boiling water to cover or steam them in a steamer basket until completely tender when poked with a fork. Drain thoroughly, then add milk and butter and mash with a potato masher until fluffy. Season with salt and pepper to taste. Spread the mashed potatoes over the meat mixture in the baking dish, patting it down and swirling with a fork or spoon for a decorative touch. A sprinkle of paprika on top is a cheery touch if you happen to have some around. Place in the oven and bake for 35 to 40 minutes, or until the top is beginning to brown and the meat mixture is bubbling underneath.

Makes 4 to 6 servings.

Steak Out!

Feeling carnivorous? Nothing satisfies a craving for pure, unadulterated meat like a good steak. Here are some pointers for buying and cooking that slab o' beef.

What kind?

If you're a cooking-steak novice, choose a boneless cut. Bones complicate the matter, so start with something simple.

For sheer beefy flavor and tenderness, and if you're willing to spend a little money, you can't go wrong with a strip loin or rib-eye steak. It should be a minimum of ¾ inch (1.5 cm) thick so that it can nicely brown on the surface without getting overcooked inside.

For a bit less cash, look for top sirloin, sirloin tip or flank steak. You'll sacrifice a little tenderness, but these all have good flavor and should do the trick. A marinade will help.

What next?

Take the steak out of the refrigerator and let it come to room temperature for about 30 minutes or so before cooking. The meat will cook more evenly if it doesn't start out freezing cold.

For a rib-eye or strip steak, just brush with olive oil and sprinkle with salt and pepper. No further glop needed.

For a sirloin or flank steak, place in a zip-top plastic bag and let it marinate (see ideas on page 83) in the refrigerator for a couple of hours before cooking. Let it come to room temperature for 30 minutes before cooking, and sprinkle with salt and pepper just before cooking.

Now to cook!

On a barbecue grill: Preheat the grill so it's nice and hot. Slap the meat on the grill and cook for about 3 minutes on each side (more if the steaks are extra thick, less if they're thin), turning over once. Cut a little slit into the middle of the meat to see if it's done to your liking— if not quite cooked enough, continue to grill in 1-minute increments until perfect. You do *not* want to overcook this thing.

With an oven broiler: Preheat the broiler for at least 5 minutes and arrange the oven rack so that the meat is no more than 3 to 4 inches (7 to 10 cm) below the heat. Place the steak on a rack over a broiler pan and cook, about 3 minutes per side, turning once, or until done just the way you like it.

Pan-grilled: You'll need a heavy skillet for this. This method will create a lot of smoke, so you'll also need a good exhaust fan. Place the skillet—very lightly oiled—over medium-high heat for 4 or 5 minutes. The pan should be really, really hot. Slap the steak on the hot pan and cook 3 or 4 minutes per side, or until done the way you like it.

Three Marinade Ideas

Mediterranean Garlic and Herb. Mix olive oil, minced or pressed garlic, fresh rosemary (if you can find some), minced onion and a little red wine if you have it. Don't worry about exact amounts—just mix everything until it smells good and add to the steaks.

Soy and Garlic. Soy sauce mixed with minced or pressed garlic, sesame oil and grated fresh ginger are all you need. Delicious.

Chili Garlic. Mix olive oil, minced or pressed garlic, minced fresh jalapeño pepper and minced green onion.

Basic Beef Stew EF DF

On a dark and stormy night, a good old bowl of beef stew is just the thing. Serve it with some decent bread and a salad and you'll feel very cozy.

1 tbsp (15 ml)	flour
½ tsp (2 ml)	salt
¼ tsp (1 ml)	pepper
2 lbs (1 kg)	beef stew meat, cut into 1-inch (2 cm) cubes (see note)
1 tbsp (15 ml)	olive oil or vegetable oil
1	onion, chopped
2 cloves	garlic, minced or pressed
¼ cup (50 ml)	beef broth or red wine (if you happen to have some)
2½ cups (625 ml)	tomato juice
2	medium carrots, cut into 1-inch (2 cm) pieces
1 tsp (5 ml)	dried thyme
2	medium potatoes, peeled and cubed

Preheat the oven to 375°F (190°C).

Combine the flour with the salt and pepper in a small bowl. Toss the cubes of meat in the flour mixture until evenly coated.

Heat the oil in an ovenproof Dutch oven or casserole with a lid, and place over medium heat. Add the beef cubes—in batches, don't crowd them—and brown them slowly, turning the meat over so that all sides are evenly colored. When all the meat is done, remove the chunks from the pot and set aside.

Add the chopped onion and garlic to the pot, and sauté just until softened—about 5 minutes. Add the broth or wine and stir to dissolve any crusty bits from the bottom of the pot. Now return the meat to the pot along with the tomato juice, carrots and thyme, and let the mixture come to a simmer. Cover the pot, place in the preheated oven and bake for 1 hour without peeking.

After 1 hour, remove the pot from the oven and add the potatoes, stirring to mix them into the liquid. Cover the pot and continue baking for at least 1 more hour, or until the meat is tender when you stick a fork in it. If it isn't, then give it another ½ hour or so and test again.

Makes 3 to 4 servings.

Stewing Beef—What Is It, Anyway?

In the supermarket you'll sometimes find packages of something labeled *stewing beef*—all conveniently cut up and ready to cook. This is usually meat cut from a less tender part of the beef and it is perfect to use in stew. If stewing beef isn't available, choose a thick chuck steak—with or without bones—and cut it into chunks yourself. (Discard the bones or save them to add to Garbage Broth—page 43.) Anything labeled shoulder, chuck, brisket, plate or blade will be good. If you're still confused, knock on the door of the supermarket meat department and ask. Butchers are usually more than happy to help you pick the right cut for what you're making.

Good Old Oven-Braised Pot Roast EF DF

Make pot roast when you expect to be hanging around the house all day. Transforming a tough hunk of meat into a delicious dinner takes a long time. While the roast is cooking, your kitchen will smell delicious.

2 tbsp (30 ml)	olive oil or vegetable oil
3 to 4 lbs (1.5 to 2 kg)	beef pot roast (see page 15 for suitable cuts), with or without bones
1 tsp (5 ml)	salt
½ tsp (2 ml)	black pepper
3	medium onions, peeled and thickly sliced
¼ cup (50 ml)	ketchup
¼ cup (50 ml)	vinegar (cider or wine vinegar is best, but white will do)
2 tbsp (30 ml)	soy sauce
2 tbsp (30 ml)	Worcestershire sauce
2 cloves	garlic, minced or pressed
1 tsp (5 ml)	crumbled rosemary or thyme or oregano (or a little of each)
2 tsp (10 ml)	prepared mustard (Dijon is nice, but use whatever you have)
3	medium potatoes, cut into large chunks
3	medium carrots, cut into 1-inch (3 cm) pieces

Preheat the oven to 350°F (180°C).

Heat the oil in a large ovenproof pot with a lid (a Dutch oven is good) over medium heat. Sprinkle the meat with the salt and pepper, and place it in the pot. Cook, turning it over several times, until all the sides of the hunk are browned and crusty.

Add the sliced onions to the pot, placing them around and on top of the meat. In a small bowl, stir together the ketchup, vinegar, soy sauce, Worcestershire sauce, garlic, rosemary (or whatever herbs you're using) and mustard. Pour this mixture over and around the meat, cover with the lid and place in the preheated oven. Let the pot roast bake—more technically speaking, *braise*—for 1½ hours, without peeking.

Add the potatoes and carrots to the pot, arranging them snugly around the meat. Put the cover back on, return pot to the oven and continue to braise for 1 to 2 hours, or until the meat is tender right through to the middle. Stick a long fork or knife into the roast—it should slide right in without any resistance when the meat is done. You want well done—not medium rare.

To serve, remove the meat from the pot, slice it thickly (it may fall apart, which is an excellent sign) and arrange it on a platter. Surround with the vegetables you fished out of the pot. Pour the pan juices into a small dish or pitcher, and serve with the meat and vegetables.

Makes 6 to 8 servings.

Fabulous Fajitas EF

Fajitas are a great way to stretch a small amount of steak to serve a bunch of people. They're also fun to make, and even more fun to eat. A win–win.

1	lime, juice squeezed
2 tbsp (30 ml)	olive oil or vegetable oil (plus more for cooking)
2 cloves	garlic, minced or pressed
½ tsp (5 ml)	cumin
1	fresh jalapeño pepper, minced (optional)
¼ cup (50 ml)	chopped cilantro
1 lb (500 g)	flank steak (or, if unavailable, sirloin)
2	medium red, green or yellow sweet peppers, sliced into thick lengthwise strips
1	large onion, sliced into thick strips
12	small (7-inch/18 cm) flour tortillas, warmed
	Fajita toppings: guacamole, salsa, sour cream, shredded cheese, shredded lettuce, whatever you like

In a small bowl, mix the lime juice, oil, garlic, cumin, jalapeño and cilantro. Place the flank steak into a zip-top plastic bag and add the lime mixture. Press as much air out of the bag as possible and zip the top shut. Smoosh the bag around to coat the meat with the marinade and refrigerate for at least 1 hour (or even overnight).

Place a large cast iron or other heavy skillet over high heat. Add a small amount of oil to the pan, then remove the steak from the bag and place in the hot skillet. Cook for about 3 minutes per side, turning once, for medium-rare meat. (Cook longer if you want it less rare.) Remove steak to a plate or cutting board while you cook the onions and peppers.

Add a little more oil to the pan and reduce the heat to medium. Toss in the onions and peppers, and cook, stirring constantly, for about 5 minutes, or until just softened.

Now have a good close look at the meat. You'll see the grain running lengthwise. With a sharp knife, cut the meat as thinly as possible across the grain. Place sliced steak on a platter and surround with onions and peppers.

Serve immediately with your choice of toppings (see above) and warmed flour tortillas. Let everyone roll their own perfect fajitas. *¡Muy bueno!*

Makes 4 servings.

Chicken option

1 lb (500 g) boneless, skinless chicken breasts, cut into strips. Same marinade. As good as the beef—maybe even better. Why not make some of each?

Note

You can grill the meat on the barbecue, or even broil it on a pan in the oven if you prefer (see Steak Out! on page 82). The peppers and onions will still have to be stir-fried in an oiled skillet, however.

Forgotten Lamb Stew EF DF

Layer all the ingredients in a Dutch oven, set it on the stove and basically forget about it. But not completely. Don't leave town or anything. Dinner will be ready in a couple of hours (or so).

2 lbs (1 kg)	boneless lamb shoulder, cut into 1-inch (2 cm) cubes
4	medium potatoes, sliced ½ inch (1 cm) thick
1	large onion, thickly sliced
2 stalks	celery, thickly sliced
4	medium carrots, peeled and thickly sliced
1 tsp (5 ml)	salt
¼ tsp (1 ml)	black pepper
½ tsp (2 ml)	thyme
1 cup (250 ml)	water
2 tbsp (30 ml)	flour
½ cup (125 ml)	cold water
2 tbsp (30 ml)	chopped fresh dill or parsley

Cut up all the ingredients, then layer them in a large pot or Dutch oven in the following order: lamb cubes, potatoes, onion, celery and, finally, carrots. Sprinkle each layer with a little of the salt, pepper and thyme.

Pour 1 cup (250 ml) water into the pot, cover pot with a tight-fitting lid and bring very slowly to a boil over medium-low heat. Lower the heat so that the mixture is just barely simmering, then go away and do your homework or something for about 2½ hours. Don't stir this while it's cooking. Really.

In a small bowl, whisk the flour into ½ cup (125 ml) of cold water to make a smooth mixture. Remove the lid of the pot, pour in the flour mixture and very gently stir the forgotten stew (try not to smash up the potatoes). Cook until the liquid has thickened. Add the dill or parsley and let cook for another minute or two. Done.

Makes about 4 servings.

Rosemary Garlic Pork Tenderloin GF EF DF

Pork tenderloin is the boneless chicken breast of pork. It's very lean, easy to cook and inexpensive when it goes on sale. One tenderloin usually weighs about 1 lb (500 g) and serves two. Double the recipe if you're feeding more people.

1 tbsp (15 ml)	olive oil or vegetable oil
1 tbsp (15 ml)	chopped fresh rosemary (or 1 tsp/5 ml dried)
2 cloves	garlic, minced or pressed
1 tsp (5 ml)	salt
¼ tsp (1 ml)	black pepper
1	pork tenderloin (about 1 lb/500 g)
1 cup (250 ml)	white wine or chicken broth (or half and half)

Preheat the oven to 400°F (200°C).

In a small bowl, mash together the oil, rosemary, garlic, salt and pepper. Smear this mixture all over the pork tenderloin. Put a large (10-inch/25 cm) ovenproof skillet on the stove over medium heat, place the tenderloin in the pan and sear the meat until it's browned on all sides—this should take about 10 minutes. (If you don't have an ovenproof skillet, just use any skillet and transfer the meat to a baking dish after browning.)

If your skillet is ovenproof, pour the wine or broth into the skillet around the meat and place it in the preheated oven. (Otherwise, transfer the tenderloin to an ovenproof baking dish before adding liquid and placing it in the oven.) Bake for 10 minutes. Remove from oven, cover the tenderloin with foil to keep warm and let rest for 10 minutes. (It's exhausted!) During this resting period, the meat will continue to cook, so don't skip this step.

Remove tenderloin to a cutting board, slice crosswise into ½-inch (1 cm) slices and serve with the sauce from the pan.

Makes 2 servings.

Unfried Chicken EF

Better than takeout, crisp, delicious, easy—why would anyone *not* make this? Buy only your favorite chicken parts—breasts, drumsticks, whichever bits you like best—or start with a whole chicken and deconstruct it yourself.

1 cup (250 ml)	dry bread crumbs
1 tbsp (15 ml)	grated Parmesan cheese
1 tsp (5 ml)	crumbled dried oregano or Italian seasoning
½ tsp (2 ml)	salt
¼ tsp (1 ml)	black pepper
2½ to 3 lbs (1 to 1.5 kg)	chicken pieces, or one medium chicken cut up
2 to 3 tbsp (30 to 45 ml)	olive oil or vegetable oil

Preheat the oven to 375°F (190°C).

In a plastic or paper bag, combine the bread crumbs, Parmesan cheese, oregano or Italian seasoning, salt and pepper. Hold the top of the bag shut and shake to mix.

Pour the vegetable oil into a small bowl and, using a basting brush or a *clean* paintbrush, brush the chicken pieces with the oil. Drop 2 or 3 pieces of chicken at a time into the bag and shake them until they are well coated with crumbs. Take them out of the bag and arrange the pieces on a rack placed over a baking sheet. (The rack allows the fat to drain from the chicken.)

When all the pieces are crumbed, place in the oven and bake for 25 minutes, then turn the pieces over and bake for another 20 to 25 minutes, or until golden brown. To be sure the chicken is properly cooked through, poke a fork into a thick section: if the juice that comes out is clear—not pink—the chicken is done.

Makes 3 or 4 servings.

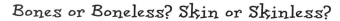

Bones or Boneless? Skin or Skinless?

Lots to choose from in the chicken section of the supermarket. If chicken bones and skin gross you out, buy boneless and skinless pieces. If, on the other hand, you like a little something to gnaw on and skin doesn't bother you, go with bone-in, skin-on chicken (it's usually the cheaper option). The recipe will work either way, but baking time will be slightly shorter for boneless pieces.

Something's Fishy with This Chicken ...

Why, it's fish, of course! Instead of chicken, try this recipe with 1 lb (500 g) fish fillets—like tilapia or haddock. Reduce the baking time to a total of 15 to 20 minutes, or until the fish flakes when you poke it with a fork.

Fancy It Up!

For something a little more special, you can turn this plain Unfried Chicken into Chicken Parmigiana in a flash. Make the recipe as above, using only boneless, skinless chicken breasts. Arrange the cooked pieces in a baking dish, heat up some spaghetti sauce and spoon a little over each piece (store-bought sauce is fine). Sprinkle with shredded mozzarella and grated Parmesan, and place in the oven (350°F/180°C) for about 10 minutes, or until the cheese is melted and the sauce is hot. Done.

How to Cut Up a Chicken

Oh yuck. You've got yourself a whole chicken and now you have to dismantle it. Although you don't need a degree in veterinary medicine to take a chicken apart, getting to know your victim before you begin is helpful.

Lay the bird out on the counter, belly up, and examine it for a couple of minutes. Move the various appendages so you can feel where the joints are and how everything hooks together. Flap the wings, walk the chicken around on its drumsticks, have it do a little chicken dance around the room. Sound effects are useful to help you get into the mood. Okay, that's enough. Now get to work.

Using a sharp knife or, better yet, a pair of good, sharp kitchen shears, cut the chicken lengthwise through the breast from the tail end to the neck end. Now open the chicken up like a book and cut alongside the backbone from one end to the other. You will have two more or less identical halves. Feeling for the joint where it attaches to the body, cut the drumstick off. There is a place where it detaches fairly easily, so keep poking around with your knife until you find the right spot. Next, remove the whole wing in a similar fashion. Finally, separate the breast from the thigh by cutting the two sections apart along the curve of the thigh section. Then, with a final whack, hack the backbone in two. There. Now do the same thing to the other half.

If you have followed these instructions, you will end up with 2 drumsticks, 2 wings, 2 breasts and 2 thighs. If you have gone berserk, you may have more pieces. You can now either cook the entire bird, or cook some of it and wrap the remaining pieces individually in plastic or foil and freeze them for a rainy day. Don't forget to label the packages!

Coconut Chicken Curry GF EF DF

All the creamy deliciousness of chicken curry with none of the usual ruckus that goes into making it. This curry is quite mild— if you want more heat, you can put in another hot pepper or sprinkle in some cayenne when you add the curry powder.

2 lbs (1 kg)	skinless, boneless chicken breasts, cut into 1-inch (2 cm) chunks
1 tsp (5 ml)	salt
½ tsp (2 ml)	black pepper
1 tbsp (15 ml)	vegetable oil
2 tbsp (30 ml)	curry powder
1	medium onion, sliced
2 cloves	garlic, minced or pressed
1	fresh jalapeño pepper, seeded and sliced (optional)
1 can (14 oz/400 ml)	coconut milk, regular or light
2 cups (500 ml)	canned diced tomatoes (or diced fresh ones)
2 tbsp (30 ml)	granulated sugar

In a bowl, toss the chicken chunks with the salt and pepper. Set aside.

In a large, deep skillet or a Dutch oven, heat the oil over medium heat. Sprinkle in the curry powder and cook, stirring constantly, for about 1 minute, or until combined. Add the onion, garlic and jalapeño pepper (if you're using it), and continue to cook, stirring to coat with spices, for 3 or 4 minutes, or until onions are beginning to soften. Dump in the chicken chunks, raise the heat to medium high and cook, stirring often, until the chicken has turned mostly opaque.

Add the coconut milk, tomatoes and sugar to the pan, bring to a boil, then lower the heat to medium and simmer, uncovered, stirring occasionally, for 15 to 20 minutes. Serve with plain, basmati or jasmine rice.

Makes about 4 servings.

Incredible Garlic Chicken GF EF DF

This recipe is not a joke. Not only is it totally delicious and very easy to make, but it is also guaranteed to protect you against vampires. An old Transylvanian recipe. Just kidding.

1	medium chicken (3 lbs/1.5 kg)
1 tsp (5 ml)	salt
½ tsp (2 ml)	black pepper
2 tbsp (30 ml)	olive oil or vegetable oil
½ tsp (2 ml)	crumbled dried thyme
1 or 2	whole bay leaves
½ cup (125 ml)	white wine or chicken broth
40 cloves	garlic—separate them, but leave the skins on (really)

Preheat the oven to 375°F (190°C).

Wash the chicken and pat it dry with a paper towel. Sprinkle inside and out (yes, it's icky in there) with salt and pepper. (Then go wash your hands.)

Heat the oil in a large skillet over medium heat. Brown the whole chicken in the hot oil, turning it repeatedly so you get all the sides. Don't worry if you miss a spot—just try to get most of the chicken golden brown. Remove the chicken from the skillet and place it in a large ovenproof casserole or Dutch oven.

Reduce the heat under the skillet to medium low and pour in the wine or broth, stirring to dissolve the browned bits from the bottom of the pan (this is called *deglazing*). Add this liquid to the casserole with the chicken.

Add the thyme and bay leaves to the chicken in the casserole and then, finally, toss in the garlic cloves. Yes, *all 40 cloves*—and *don't* peel them. Trust me.

Cover the casserole tightly with a lid (or use foil if you don't have a lid that fits), and bake in the preheated oven for 1¼ to 1½ hours. And *don't peek* while the chicken is cooking.

Remove the casserole from the oven, carefully lift the lid and inhale the amazing aroma. Cut the chicken into pieces and serve along with the cooked garlic cloves and some of the delicious sauce. The garlic will have turned squishy and sweet, and it's fantastic when spread on some good crusty bread (or just sucked out of its skin). (Eat a handful of parsley before going out in public.)

Makes 3 or 4 servings.

Good Old Roast Chicken GF EF DF

Almost everyone likes roast chicken. It's familiar, delicious and very homey. Plus it makes for great leftovers the next day—if there are any leftovers, that is.

1	medium to large chicken (3 to 4 lbs/1.5 to 2 kg)
2 cloves	garlic, minced or pressed
1 tbsp (15 ml)	olive oil or vegetable oil
1 tsp (5 ml)	salt
1 tsp (5 ml)	paprika
½ tsp (2 ml)	pepper

Preheat the oven to 375°F (190°C).

Rinse the chicken under cold running water, inside and out, and dry it with paper towels. In a small bowl, mash together the garlic, oil, salt, paprika and pepper, stirring to make a fairly thick paste.

By hand or with a basting brush (if you have such a thing), rub the garlic paste all over the chicken, inside and outside. (Pretend you're applying sunscreen at the beach.) At this point, *some* people would truss the bird up with string—tying the legs together and the wings in tight to the body. The idea is to make the bird into a nice tight package so that there are no outlying appendages to overcook. But trussing isn't absolutely essential. You *can* get away without it.

Put the chicken into a roasting pan—an oblong baking pan or even a disposable foil pan—and roast, uncovered, for 1½ to 2 hours, basting with the pan juices occasionally, until the chicken is a deep golden brown and the leg moves easily when you jiggle it. When you stab the chicken with a fork, the juices that run out should be clear, not pink. If you're still not sure whether it's done, poke an instant-read meat thermometer into a thick part of the thigh (not touching the bone). If the thermometer reads 165°F (74°C), the chicken is done.

Remove from the oven and let rest for about 5 minutes before cutting it up. It will be easier to handle and won't leak quite as much.

Serves, oh, maybe 3 or 4, depending on who you're feeding and exactly how big the chicken is.

 # Chicken Cacciatore EF DF

This saucy Italian classic is guaranteed to warm up the chilliest winter evening. Spoon it over some pasta, add a crusty loaf of bread and a nice salad, and it's *perfecto*.

1	medium chicken (3 lbs/1.5 kg) cut up into serving pieces, or 3 lbs/1.5 kg of chicken thighs
2 tbsp (30 ml)	all-purpose flour
½ tsp (2 ml)	salt
¼ tsp (1 ml)	black pepper
1 tbsp (15 ml)	olive oil or vegetable oil
1	medium onion, chopped
1	sweet green pepper, chopped
8 oz (250 g)	fresh mushrooms, thickly sliced (about 2 cups/500 ml sliced)
2 cloves	garlic, minced or pressed
1 tsp (5 ml)	crumbled dried oregano
½ tsp (2 ml)	crumbled dried thyme
1 can (28 oz/796 ml)	diced tomatoes
½ cup (125 ml)	chicken broth (prepared broth or made from bouillon cube or powder)
¼ cup (75 ml)	tomato paste (about half a 5.5 oz/156 ml can)
⅓ cup (50 ml)	chopped fresh parsley
	Additional salt and pepper if needed

Trim all the excess fat and hangy skin from the chicken pieces and discard. Place the chicken in a large bowl, sprinkle with the flour, salt and pepper and toss to coat evenly with the flour.

In a Dutch oven or large saucepan with a lid, heat the oil over medium-high heat. Working with just 3 or 4 pieces at a time, brown the chicken in the hot oil, turning over to brown all sides well. Remove chicken pieces to a plate once they're browned and continue until all the pieces are done.

Pour out all except for about 1 tbsp (15 ml) of the fat from the pot. Add the onion, pepper, mushrooms, garlic, oregano and thyme, and cook, stirring occasionally, until the vegetables are softened—about 6 to 8 minutes. Add the tomatoes, broth and tomato paste, and bring the mixture to a boil. Add browned chicken pieces to the sauce, then turn the heat down to low and cook, covered, for 20 to 25 minutes, stirring occasionally. Taste, and adjust seasoning with salt and pepper if needed. Sprinkle with chopped parsley and serve immediately.

Makes 4 servings.

Not Your Mom's Chicken Stew with Dumplings EF

If your mom made chicken stew with dumplings, this recipe is probably not the same as hers. But this one is good, it's easy and (most important) it has dumplings. What more could you possibly want?

4	skinless, boneless chicken breasts
4	medium potatoes, peeled and cut into 1-inch (2 cm) chunks
4	carrots, cut into 1-inch (2 cm) chunks
3 stalks	celery, cut into 1-inch (2 cm) pieces
2	onions, diced
4 cups (1 l)	chicken broth (prepared broth or made from bouillon cubes or powder)
1 tbsp (15 ml)	chopped fresh parsley
1 tsp (5 ml)	salt
¼ tsp (1 ml)	black pepper
1 cup (250 ml)	frozen peas
¾ cup (175 ml)	all-purpose flour
¼ cup (50 ml)	cornmeal
2 tsp (10 ml)	baking powder
¼ tsp (1 ml)	salt
2 tbsp (30 ml)	olive oil or vegetable oil
½ cup (125 ml)	milk

In a large saucepan or Dutch oven, combine the chicken, potatoes, carrots, celery and onions. Add the chicken broth, parsley, salt and pepper, and bring to a boil over high heat. Reduce the heat to medium low, cover the pot and let the stew simmer for 20 minutes. Stir in the peas.

Meanwhile, in a medium bowl, mix the flour, cornmeal, baking powder and salt. Stir in the milk and oil, and mix just until everything is thoroughly moistened.

Lift the lid of the pot and drop the dumpling batter into the simmering stew by tablespoons—there should be 6 to 8 blobs. Re-cover the pot and cook for 15 minutes. Don't lift the lid, don't peek, don't do anything. It will be fine, I promise.

Makes 4 very comforting servings.

Curry Glazed Chicken EF

What a dilemma. You want to appear sophisticated, worldly, slightly daring. But at the same time, you don't want to go too far, because maybe your dinner guest isn't particularly sophisticated, worldly or daring. You'll need to compromise. Try this.

1 tbsp (15 ml)	butter
¼ cup (50 ml)	honey
3 tbsp (45 ml)	Dijon mustard
2 tsp (10 ml)	curry powder
½ tsp (2 ml)	salt
1	medium chicken (3 lbs/1.5 kg) cut up into serving pieces (or 3 lbs/1.5 kg your choice of any chicken parts)

Preheat the oven to 375°F (190°C).

Measure the butter into a 9 x 13-inch (23 x 33 cm) rectangular baking dish and put it into the oven to melt.

When the butter is melted, remove the pan from the oven and stir in the honey, the mustard, the curry powder and the salt. Add the chicken pieces to the pan, turning them over to coat with the honey mixture on all sides.

Bake for 45 minutes, turning the chicken pieces over about halfway through the baking time.

Serve with something that will sop up the delicious sauce—like rice, couscous or quinoa.

Makes 3 or 4 servings.

Honey Garlic Wings GF EF DF

If you eat these wings with your hands, sitting in front of the TV, they're a snack. On a plate, at the table—they're a meal. Either way, these wings are delicious.

3 lbs (1.5 kg)	chicken wings
4 cloves	garlic, peeled
1 cup (250 ml)	honey or brown sugar
½ cup (125 ml)	water
¼ cup (50 ml)	soy sauce
1 tbsp (15 ml)	vinegar
1 tsp (5 ml)	ground ginger

Preheat the oven to 375°F (190°C).

Trim the pointy tips off each wing and discard them, or save to add to chicken soup (page 47) or garbage broth (page 43). Cut each wing in half at the elbow. Arrange wings in single layer in a baking dish just large enough to hold them all.

In a food processor or blender, combine the garlic, honey or brown sugar, water, soy sauce, vinegar and ginger. Whirl until smooth. Pour this mixture over the wings and toss them to coat. Bake for 15 minutes, turn the wings over in the sauce and continue to bake for another 15 to 20 minutes, or until the wings are browned and the sauce is nice and sticky.

Eat them just like that—straight from the pan. Or be a grown-up about it and serve them on a plate with some rice to sop up the extra sauce.

Makes 3 to 4 servings. Or less.

Thermonuclear Buffalo Wings EF

Traditionally served with celery sticks and blue cheese dressing, these wings are an easy version of the Buffalo classic. To avoid Total Meltdown, you may, if absolutely necessary, reduce the amount of hot pepper sauce. Or not. Your choice.

2 lbs (kg)	chicken wings (about 12)
½ cup (125 ml)	all-purpose flour
½ tsp (2 ml)	pepper
¼ cup (50 ml)	butter
3 tbsp (45 ml)	hot pepper sauce (*less* for the timid, *more* for the brave)
1 tbsp (15 ml)	white or cider vinegar

Preheat the oven to 375°F (190°C).

Trim the pointy tips off each wing and discard them, or save to add to chicken soup (page 47) or garbage broth (page 43). Cut each wing in half at the elbow. Put the flour and salt into a small bag, toss in 3 or 4 wings at a time, hold the top closed and shake until coated. Remove the floured wings to a baking pan or cookie sheet and repeat until all the wings are done. Bake for 15 minutes, then turn the wings over and bake another 15 to 20 minutes, or until crisp and browned.

While the wings are baking, melt the butter with the hot pepper sauce and the vinegar in a small saucepan. Stir to mix, and remove from heat. As soon as the wings are done, remove them to a bowl, drizzle with the hot sauce mixture and toss to coat.

Serve immediately.

Makes 12 wings—between 1 and 3 servings, depending.

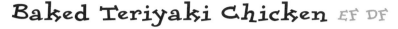

Baked Teriyaki Chicken EF DF

Something magically delicious happens when homemade teriyaki sauce meets chicken pieces.

½ cup (125 ml)	soy sauce
½ cup (125 ml)	granulated sugar
¼ cup (50 ml)	cider or white vinegar
1 tbsp (15 ml)	cornstarch
2 cloves	garlic, minced or pressed
1 tsp (5 ml)	ground ginger (or 1 tbsp/15 ml grated fresh gingerroot)
¼ tsp (1 ml)	black pepper
2 lbs (500 g)	skinless, boneless chicken thighs, cut in half
1 tbsp (15 ml)	sesame seeds

Preheat the oven to 375°F (190°C).

Grease a 9 x 13-inch (23 x 33 cm) rectangular baking dish or, for easier cleanup, line the baking dish with foil and grease the foil.

In a small saucepan, stir together the soy sauce, sugar, vinegar, cornstarch, garlic, ginger and pepper. Mix well to eliminate any lumps of cornstarch, then place over medium heat and cook, stirring constantly, until the sauce bubbles and becomes thick and glossy.

Arrange the chicken thigh pieces in the prepared baking dish, pour in the teriyaki sauce and mix everything to coat the chicken evenly. Place in the preheated oven and bake for 45 minutes to 1 hour, turning and rearranging the chicken pieces and basting with sauce every 15 minutes, until cooked through and nicely glazed.

Sprinkle with sesame seeds and serve chicken with rice, couscous or quinoa to sop up the delicious sauce.

Makes about 4 servings.

# Cooking a Whole Turkey GF EF DF

Cooking a whole turkey isn't a crazy thing to do. Turkey is cheap, delicious and easy to cook. Leftover turkey makes the world's best sandwich (with plenty of mayo) and the bones are great for soup. If you're afraid of tackling an entire turkey, practice on a chicken first (see recipe on page 95). A chicken is the same thing, only smaller.

How to Thaw a Frozen Turkey

Leaving a frozen turkey out on the kitchen counter to thaw at room temperature is an excellent way to breed the sorts of bacteria you might study in science class but you certainly don't want to eat. Here are a couple of safe ways to deal with that frozen hunk.

Option 1. Leave the frozen, plastic-wrapped turkey in your refrigerator for a day or two. It will eventually thaw. But this method is not fast, so if you're in a hurry, try option 2.

Option 2. Place the frozen, plastic-wrapped turkey in the kitchen sink and fill the sink with enough cold water to cover the bird. Drain the sink and refill with fresh cold water every so often until the turkey is thawed. This is a safe, quick method as long as you don't forget about the turkey and accidentally leave it there overnight.

A fresh (not frozen) turkey will just need to be washed and patted dry before you proceed.

Whether you've bought frozen or fresh, make sure you check inside the cavity for that cute little surprise packet (liver, heart, other innards). Remove it and use the contents to make soup, feed to the cat or pull a juvenile practical joke on a friend.

1	turkey, any size, washed and patted dry
2 tbsp (30 ml)	olive oil or vegetable oil
4 cloves	garlic, minced or pressed
2 tsp (10 ml)	salt
2 tsp (10 ml)	paprika
1 tsp (5 ml)	black pepper

In a small bowl, mash together the oil, garlic, salt, paprika and pepper. By hand, or with a brush (if you're the squeamish type), apply this mixture to the turkey, inside and out, the way you'd smear sunscreen on at the beach. Stuff the turkey if you want (see recipe, page 104) or leave it unstuffed.

Tie the turkey's legs together with some string, and tie the wings in close to the body. The idea is to make as compact a package as possible so that there are no sticking-out parts to overcook before the rest of the turkey is done.

Place the turkey in an open roasting pan and roast it in a 350°F (180°C) oven. For the first hour, baste the turkey often (every 10 minutes or so) with some oil or melted butter. Once the juices start to seep out and collect in the bottom of the pan, you can use them to baste the bird—and keep basting every 20 minutes, or whenever you think of it. Basting helps keep the turkey moist and it gives the turkey that nice crunchy skin everyone loves. Cooking time will depend on the size of your turkey:

Roasting times at 350°F (180°C):

Weight	Roasting time lbs (kg)	
	stuffed	unstuffed
6 to 8 lbs (3 to 4 kg)	2½ to 3 hours	2 to 2½ hours
10 to 12 lbs (4.5 to 5.5 kg)	4 hours (or more)	3 to 3½ hours
14 to 18 lbs (6 to 8 kg)	5 to 6 hours	3½ to 4 hours
18 lbs and up (8 kg +)	6 hours (or more)	4 hours (or more)

When the turkey is done, the leg will wiggle easily and the juices will run clear when you poke the bird with a knife, and if you happen to have a meat thermometer (yes!), it will register 165 to 170°F (74 to 76°C) in the thickest part of the thigh. Remove the bird from the oven and let rest (it's had a hard day) for 15 to 20 minutes before scooping the stuffing out (if you've made it) and carving the meat.

Spoon the pan juices into a bowl and serve them with the turkey just the way they are. Or you may want to make a proper gravy (see recipe on page 105) while the turkey is resting.

Oh, and don't forget the cranberry sauce.

Important Safety Bulletin!

Never leave stuffing inside a turkey for any length of time, either before or after it has been cooked. The interior of a turkey is an amazing breeding ground for the kind of bacteria you don't want to feed to anyone you like. Stuff a turkey just before it goes into the oven and remove the stuffing promptly after the bird is done. This is not a joke.

Stuffing—the Best Part of the Turkey DF

The next time you're at a turkey dinner, watch to see what people eat first. Hint: it's not the brussels sprouts.

¼ cup (50 ml)	olive oil or vegetable oil
1	onion, chopped
1 stalk	celery, finely chopped
8 cups (2 l)	slightly stale bread, torn by hand into rough bits
¼ cup (50 ml)	finely chopped fresh parsley
1 tbsp (15 ml)	crumbled dried sage or poultry seasoning
½ tsp (2 ml)	salt
¼ tsp (1 ml)	black pepper

Heat the oil in a small skillet, add the onion and celery, and sauté for 5 to 8 minutes, until softened.

In a large bowl, combine the crumbled bread, the sage or poultry seasoning, parsley, salt and pepper. Add the onion mixture and toss to combine. Taste to see if it needs any more salt or pepper, then stuff into the cavity of the turkey before tying it up with string. You can bake any extra stuffing separately in a greased casserole dish.

This recipe makes enough stuffing for an 8 to 10 lb (4 to 5 kg) turkey. You can double the recipe for a larger bird, and there's no law that says you can't use it with chicken.

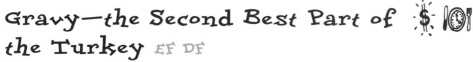

Gravy—the Second Best Part of the Turkey EF DF

You'll have enough time to make this gravy while the turkey is resting after you pull it out of the oven.

2 tbsp (30 ml)	fat from the roasting pan
2 tbsp (30 ml)	all-purpose flour
2 cups (500 ml)	turkey broth, chicken broth or, if all else fails, water

After your turkey is finished roasting, remove it from the roasting pan and place it on a large carving board or platter. Pour or spoon all the pan juices into a bowl and let them settle for a few minutes. Meanwhile, pour the broth or water into the (now empty) roasting pan and swish it around to dissolve the delicious crusty stuff on the bottom of the pan. (We're *deglazing* here.)

Now back to the pan juices. With a spoon, skim off as much of the fat that has risen to the top as you possibly can. Take 2 tbsp (30 ml) of that fat and place it in a small saucepan. Discard the rest of the fat, but hang on to the pan juices. Add the flour to the fat in the saucepan and stir to blend. Place over medium heat and cook, stirring, for a minute or two. Pour in the reserved pan juices and the broth used to deglaze the roasting pan. Cook over medium heat, stirring constantly, until thickened—at least 5 minutes.

Makes about 2 cups (500 ml) of the best gravy you will ever taste.

Fried Rice with Whatever GF DF

Fried rice—a brilliant invention—is best when made with cold leftover rice and whatever bits of stuff you happen to have in your fridge. Vegetarians can just skip the meat and double the vegetables or use firm tofu in place of the meat.

2 tbsp (30 ml)	vegetable oil
1	onion, chopped
2 cloves	garlic, minced or pressed
1	egg, beaten
2 cups (500 ml)	diced or sliced fresh, frozen or cooked vegetables (any mixture of whatever you have around—celery, green pepper, mushrooms, carrots, bean sprouts, green beans, broccoli, zucchini, peas, baby spinach leaves)
2 cups (500 ml)	diced cooked meat or fish of any kind (chicken, beef, pork, shrimp, turkey, groundhog and so on)
3 cups (750 ml)	leftover cooked rice
2 tbsp (30 ml)	soy sauce
1 tsp (5 ml)	sesame oil (if you have it—it's very nice)
4	green onions, sliced

In a wok or a large skillet, heat the oil over high heat. Add the onion and garlic, and stir-fry for 1 or 2 minutes, until the onion is slightly softened. Stir in the egg and cook the mixture just until the egg is scrambled—this will only take a minute. Toss in the vegetables— whatever you're using—the ones that take the longest time to cook first, then the next, and the next, and the next, adding any *cooked* vegetables only at the last minute. Generally, soft watery vegetables (like zucchini and bean sprouts) will cook faster than hard solid ones (like carrots and celery). But really, don't go all technical about this. It isn't rocket science—it's just dinner.

When the vegetables are all in the wok, throw in the meat and stir everything a bit. Since this ingredient is already cooked, you just need to heat it. Now add the rice and keep stirring. Add the soy sauce and cook the whole business, stirring and tossing, for 2 or 3 minutes, until everything is hot and well mixed. Sprinkle in the sesame oil, if you're using it, and the green onions. Toss it all around, remove from heat and serve immediately.

Serves 3 or 4 as a main dish.

Dribs-and-Drabs Stir-Fry

This is not a recipe. Well, not exactly. Only you know what dribs and drabs lurk in the darkest recesses of your refrigerator. Half a withered onion. Two pitiful carrots. A pathetic, lonesome, partially eaten chicken leg. Seven green beans (why did you keep seven green beans?). This sorry collection is about to turn into dinner. Really.

Start by cutting up everything you can find into smallish pieces—arrange these attractively on a large platter (or a couple of plates). Put all the cooked stuff (leftover pot roast, yesterday's broccoli, half a can of corn niblets) together on one plate since these won't require as much stir-frying as the raw stuff (hunk of green pepper, slab of cabbage, sliver of bacon). The stir-fry is already starting to feel like something, isn't it?

Now make up a sauce. In a small bowl, stir together 2 tsp (10 ml) cornstarch, 2 tbsp (30 ml) soy sauce and ½ cup (125 ml) water, broth or vegetable juice (like the liquid from a can of peas or something).

Okay. Start frying. Heat 2 tbsp (30 ml) of vegetable oil in a wok or a large skillet over high heat. Definitely throw in some chopped or sliced onion to start. This always smells productive. Now add the raw stuff—meat first, if you've got some, then the hard vegetables (like carrots), then the softer things (like mushrooms). Stir-fry, tossing constantly, until the meat is cooked and the vegetables are looking hopeful. Now add the cooked bits, a little at a time until everything is in, and stir-fry for a couple of minutes more.

Stir the sauce mixture (the cornstarch will have settled to the bottom of the bowl) and add it all at once to the skillet. Cook, stirring constantly, for about a minute, until slightly thickened and bubbly. Remove from the heat and serve over hot cooked rice or pasta.

Wow. And you thought there was nothing in the house to eat.

The Leftover Zone

Leftovers are your friends. They are always there for you, waiting patiently in the fridge, ready for you to eat at any moment. Why do we treat them so badly? Here are some ways to show those loyal leftovers how much we really appreciate them.

Heat them up and serve just the way you did the first time around.
In most cases, a microwave does this best—retaining most of the taste and texture of the original.

Don't bother to heat them up.
Discover how the flavor of a hot food changes when it's cold. Cold leftover pizza actually makes a good, quick breakfast.

Make a sandwich out of them.
Meat loaf, chicken, meatballs, pot roast—they all make an excellent sandwich if you slice them thin enough and add some lettuce, tomato, onion, pickle, mayonnaise, mustard, whatever. Allegedly, leftover spaghetti makes a great sandwich, but no one has yet confirmed this scientifically.

Give them another life altogether.
Reincarnate those potatoes as a potato salad. Turn those leftover vegetables into soup. Give those shreds of chicken or turkey new life as a stir-fry. Create a brand-new dinner from old food—you *can* make a silk purse out of a sow's ear. Or, at the very least, a casserole.

Create a do-it-yourself TV dinner.
Recycle that multi-compartment plate (the kind you get with a frozen dinner) by filling it with the leftovers of a previously loved meal. Mashed potatoes here, a slice or two of meat loaf there, a few pieces of broccoli in the corner—cover with foil and freeze for another day.

(Hint: don't freeze the salad. You've been warned.)

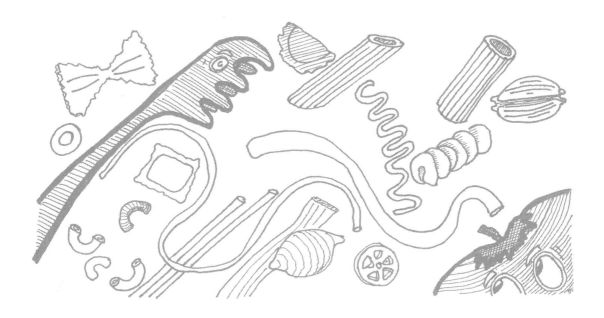

Primarily Pasta

Pasta Basics

Just exactly how much pasta is too much? Or worse, how much is too little? And how do you cook the stuff?

For one serving

- Long pasta, like spaghetti, fettuccine and linguine: a bunch ¾ inch (2 cm) in diameter
- Regular-size macaroni, like elbows, small shells, fusilli: 1 cup (250 ml)
- Larger macaroni, like rotini, large shells, rigatoni: 1⅔ cup (400 ml)
- Noodles—fine, medium and wide: 1⅔ cup (400 ml)

Shortcut

Macaroni will approximately double in volume when cooked. So if you think you can eat a whole bowlful of macaroni, fill the bowl halfway with the dry pasta and that should end up being about right.

Cooking the stuff

Fill your largest pot with water, add a spoonful of salt and bring to a full boil over high heat. If you cover the pot, the water will boil faster. Uncover, and add the pasta to the boiling water—the water will stop boiling temporarily because the pasta lowers the water temperature. Stir until the water returns to a boil to prevent the pasta sticking to the bottom of the pot, then cook until done, stirring occasionally. Don't cover the pot when cooking pasta—that can cause a messy boil-over.

How can you tell when it's done?

Small thin pasta will cook more quickly than big fat pasta. Start tasting after 5 minutes. The pasta should be tender but still a little chewy through the middle (in Italian this is called *al dente,* meaning "to the tooth"). If you're cooking spaghetti, you can use the ever-popular Wall Test: throw a strand against the wall, and if it sticks, it's done. (This test is not recommended, however, for stucco walls or when neat-freak parents or roommates are watching.)

Drain the pasta thoroughly in a strainer or colander and dump it immediately into a serving bowl or back into the cooking pot to toss with your sauce. Do not rinse the cooked pasta unless you need to cool it quickly to use in another recipe—like pasta salad or a macaroni casserole.

Pasta trivia

Adding a spoonful of oil to the cooking water does absolutely nothing useful, no matter what anyone tells you. It does not prevent the pasta from sticking together, and it does not prevent the pot from boiling over. Better to keep an eye on the stove and not overcook.

Salt doesn't help the water boil faster. It does, however, make the water salty and enhance the flavor of the cooked pasta. Or you can just add salt when you're saucing the pasta. Either way works.

If your pot starts to boil over, just blow hard over the surface and it will settle down. Meanwhile, lower the heat slightly to keep that from happening again.

Don't get stuck in a pasta rut. Elbows and spaghetti aren't the only things out there, you know. Have you ever tried fusilli? Or radiatore? Or farfalle? Each shape tastes different. Go ahead—see for yourself.

Big Batch Spaghetti Sauce GF EF DF

Every summer, millions of innocent tomatoes wither and rot simply because they have no one to love them and take care of them. This senseless waste must stop! Go seek out a big basket of perfectly ripe tomatoes, bring it home and make a vat of spaghetti sauce.

¼ cup (50 ml)	olive oil or vegetable oil
2	onions, chopped
4 to 6 cloves	garlic, minced or pressed
3 quarts (3 l)	chopped ripe tomatoes, peeled or not (see page 110)
2 tbsp (30 ml)	tomato paste
1 tsp (5 ml)	salt
½ tsp (2 ml)	black pepper
½ cup (125 ml)	chopped fresh herbs—parsley, basil, oregano, whatever (or 1 tbsp/15 ml each dried basil and oregano)

In your largest pot, heat the oil and sauté the onions and garlic over medium heat for 5 to 7 minutes, or until softened. Dump in the chopped tomatoes and bring to a boil, stirring often. Add the tomato paste, salt and pepper, and leave the whole business to simmer (no lid) for about an hour, stirring occasionally to prevent the sauce from scorching and sticking to the bottom of the pot.

When the sauce is nearly thick enough, add the fresh or dried herbs and simmer for another 15 minutes or so. Your homemade sauce may not be as thick as store-bought spaghetti sauce—after all, you aren't using any starches or thickeners. If you really think your sauce is too thin, add a bit more tomato paste, and cook until blended and thickened.

Use this sauce immediately over pasta or in lasagna, or pack into plastic containers and freeze.

Even Bigger Batch Spaghetti Sauce

Yes! You can double or triple this recipe if you want to! Just remember—the bigger the batch, the more time it will take to cook and thicken.

Chopping Tomatoes

The fastest way to chop up a lot of ripe tomatoes is to put them in a big bowl and mush them up with your bare hands. Just dive in there and squish away to your heart's content. Totally gross, very effective, really fun.

Chicken and Mushroom Pasta EF DF

Skinless and boneless chicken breasts are convenient and easy to cook. But if you have a little time to mess around, you may be able to save money by buying bone-in, skin-on chicken breasts and dismantling them yourself. You'll need about 2 lbs (1 kg) with bones and skin. Make broth with the bones and you've saved even more cash! (See Garbage Broth, page 43.)

1 lb (500 g)	skinless, boneless chicken breasts, cut into ½-inch (1 cm) cubes, more or less
1 tbsp (15 ml)	olive oil or vegetable oil
1	onion, chopped
1½ cups (375 ml)	sliced mushrooms
2 cups (500 ml)	diced tomatoes (from a can or fresh tomatoes)
1 cup (250 ml)	chicken broth (prepared broth or made from bouillon cubes or powder)
1 tsp (5 ml)	dried basil (or 1 tbsp/15 ml chopped fresh basil if you have it)
1 tsp (5 ml)	salt
¼ tsp (1 ml)	black pepper
2 cups (500 ml)	smallish pasta—shells, bow ties, fusilli, elbows

Heat the oil in a large skillet over medium heat, add the chicken cubes and cook, stirring constantly, until the meat is no longer pink—about 5 to 7 minutes. Remove the meat from the skillet, leaving as much of the oil in the pan as possible.

Add the onion and mushrooms to the skillet, and cook over medium heat until softened, about 5 minutes. Add the tomatoes, broth, basil, salt and pepper, bring to a boil, then add the (uncooked) pasta. Cover with a lid, and cook over low heat for 8 to 10 minutes, until the pasta is done, stirring occasionally.

Return the chicken to the pan, and cook for about 5 minutes, just until everything is heated through.

Makes about 4 servings.

Spicy Peanut Chicken Pasta EF DF

Go ahead—add more stuff to this if you want. Canned baby corn, fresh snow peas, some bean sprouts—they're all good.

1 lb (500 g)	boneless, skinless chicken breasts, cut into ½-inch (1 cm) cubes
1 tbsp (15 ml)	vegetable oil
1 cup (250 ml)	chicken broth (prepared broth or made from bouillon cubes or powder)
¼ cup (50 ml)	peanut butter—smooth or chunky
2 tbsp (30 ml)	honey
1 tbsp (15 ml)	soy sauce
1 tbsp (15 ml)	cornstarch
1 tsp (5 ml)	ground ginger
½ tsp (2 ml)	hot pepper flakes (or more, or less, or whatever)
2	green onions, sliced
2 cloves	garlic, minced or pressed
1	medium sweet green or red pepper, thinly sliced

Heat the vegetable oil in a large skillet over high heat, add the chicken cubes and stir-fry until lightly browned—5 to 7 minutes. Remove the chicken from the pan.

In a bowl, whisk together the chicken broth, peanut butter, honey, soy sauce, cornstarch, ginger and hot pepper flakes. Pour this mixture into the skillet and cook, stirring constantly, until thickened and smooth. Add the green onions, garlic and green or red pepper, and cook for another couple of minutes. Return the chicken pieces (and any juice from them) to the pan and simmer the mixture for 2 or 3 minutes, or until heated through.

Serve over hot cooked pasta—thin spaghetti, linguine or freshly cooked Asian noodles are all good.

Makes enough for 4 servings of pasta.

Tuna Tomato Pasta EF DF

Cheap, delicious and much more satisfying than a tuna sandwich for dinner.

2 tbsp (30 ml)	olive oil
3 cloves	garlic, minced or pressed
1 can (28 oz/796 ml)	diced tomatoes
1 can (6.5 oz/184 g)	tuna, drained
½ tsp (2 ml)	dried oregano
½ tsp (2 ml)	dried basil
½ tsp (2 ml)	red pepper flakes
½ tsp (2 ml)	salt
1 tbsp (15 ml)	capers (optional, but nice if you have them)

Heat the oil in a large skillet over medium heat. Add the garlic and sauté for about a minute, until softened but not browned. Dump in the tomatoes, tuna, oregano, basil, red pepper flakes, salt and capers, and stir. Bring to a boil, then lower the heat and simmer for 10 to 15 minutes, until the flavors are blended and the sauce has thickened a bit.

Toss with hot cooked pasta and sprinkle with lots of grated Parmesan cheese if you want.

Makes enough sauce for 4 servings of pasta.

Simple Garlic Tomato Sauce EF DF

Nothing in the house to eat? Think again. If you have a can of tomatoes, a head of garlic and some pasta, you've got dinner. You can leave the parsley out if you don't have it. Or substitute fresh basil if it's available.

4 cloves	garlic, chopped
¼ cup (50 ml)	olive oil or vegetable oil
½ cup (125 ml)	chopped fresh parsley, divided
1 can (28 oz/796 ml)	diced tomatoes
1 tsp (5 ml)	salt
½ tsp (2 ml)	black pepper

Heat the oil in a medium saucepan over medium-low heat. Add the garlic and cook, stirring often, until very soft but not brown—6 to 8 minutes. Add half the parsley and cook, stirring, for another 5 minutes until the parsley is wilted.

Pour in the tomatoes, squishing them with a wooden spoon to mash them up. Let this simmer for a long time—maybe half an hour to 45 minutes, stirring occasionally. The sauce should thicken slowly but still be a little chunky. When you think it's just about done, add the rest of the parsley, the salt and the pepper, cook for 3 to 5 minutes and serve. Toss with hot drained spaghetti or fettuccine. A sprinkle of cheese is nice.

Makes enough sauce for 4 servings of pasta.

Bolognese Sauce

What's with the fancy name, you ask? Heck, this is just regular meat spaghetti sauce. Well, whatever.

2 tbsp (30 ml)	olive oil
1	medium onion, chopped
1	medium carrot, chopped
1 stalk	celery, chopped
2 cloves	garlic, minced or pressed
1 lb (500 g)	lean ground beef
½ lb (250 g)	Italian sausage, hot or sweet, skins removed
1 can (28 oz/796 ml)	diced tomatoes
1 cup (250 ml)	beef broth (prepared broth or made from bouillon cubes or powder)
	Salt and pepper to taste

In a large saucepan or Dutch oven, heat the olive oil over medium heat. Add the onion, carrot, celery and garlic, and cook, stirring often, for about 10 minutes, or until vegetables are softened. Add the ground beef and the sausage meat, and continue to cook, stirring to break up the lumps, until the meat is no longer pink at all—8 to 10 minutes. Now add the tomatoes and the broth, bring to a boil, then reduce the heat to low. Cook, covered, for about 2 hours. Stir occasionally to make sure the sauce is not sticking on the bottom. After about 1 hour, taste the sauce and add salt and pepper if you think the sauce needs it. (The sausage and the broth may already have provided plenty of seasoning, so take it easy.)

Serve this fantastic sauce over hot cooked pasta, sprinkled with Parmesan cheese. Or use it in your own homemade lasagna (page 124) or baked pasta casserole.

Makes about 6 cups (1.5 l).

Eggplant Pasta Sauce EF DF

Eggplants are mysterious. Deep. Inscrutable. Make this dish and you will be too.

1	medium eggplant, peeled and cut into ½-inch (1 cm) cubes
1 tsp (5 ml)	salt
¼ cup (50 ml)	olive oil or vegetable oil, divided
1	large onion, chopped
2 cloves	garlic, minced or pressed
2 cups (500 ml)	diced tomatoes (canned or fresh)
1 tbsp (15 ml)	chopped fresh parsley
1 tbsp (15 ml)	chopped fresh basil (or 1 tsp/5 ml dried)
1 tsp (5 ml)	sugar
	Salt and black pepper to taste

Place the eggplant cubes in a colander or strainer set over a bowl and sprinkle with salt. Toss to coat, then let drain for an hour or so. Pat the cubes dry with paper towel and discard the liquid that has seeped out. (Salting removes some of the excess water from the eggplant so that it cooks faster and doesn't absorb as much oil. But if you're in a big rush, you can skip this step.)

Heat half the oil in a large skillet over medium-high heat. Add the eggplant cubes and cook, stirring often, until golden—5 to 7 minutes. Remove from the pan. Add the rest of the oil to the pan, then the onion and garlic, and cook, stirring, until softened—about 5 minutes. Return the eggplant to the skillet and add the tomatoes, parsley, basil and sugar. Lower the heat and simmer the sauce, uncovered, for about 10 minutes. Taste, and season with salt and pepper if needed. Serve over hot cooked pasta, sprinkled with Parmesan cheese.

Makes enough sauce for 4 servings of pasta.

Rotini with Broccoli EF

Fast, delicious and, when broccoli is on sale, a very cheap dinner.

4 cups (1 l)	uncooked rotini (or similar) pasta
1 bunch	broccoli, stalks peeled and sliced and top cut into florets
2 tbsp (30 ml)	olive oil or vegetable oil
4 cloves	garlic, squished
2 cups (500 ml)	diced tomatoes (canned or fresh)
¼ cup (50 ml)	chopped fresh parsley
½ cup (125 ml)	grated Parmesan cheese
½ tsp (2 ml)	salt
¼ tsp (1 ml)	black pepper

Cook the rotini in plenty of boiling water until done. Drain, and rinse under running water to prevent it from sticking together. Set aside.

In a steamer basket (or colander) over boiling water, steam the broccoli until just tender but still bright green and slightly crisp—7 to 10 minutes. As soon as it's done, remove from the steamer and set aside.

Heat the oil in a large skillet over medium-high heat. Add the garlic, and sauté for a minute or 2, just until softened. Add the tomatoes and parsley, and cook for 5 minutes, until the tomatoes are softened. Throw in the broccoli and toss around for a couple of minutes until everything is heated through. Stir in the rotini, sprinkle with Parmesan cheese, season with salt and pepper and serve immediately.

Makes 4 servings.

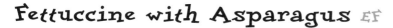

Fettuccine with Asparagus EF

This is where asparagus wants to go when it dies. Asparagus nirvana. Save this killer recipe for a special occasion.

½ cup (125 ml)	whipping cream
¼ cup (50 ml)	butter, softened to room temperature
1 cup (250 ml)	grated Parmesan cheese
1 lb (500 g)	asparagus, trimmed and cut in 1-inch (2 cm) pieces
2 tbsp (30 ml)	olive oil
2	green onions, sliced
1 lb (500 g)	uncooked fettuccine
½ tsp (2 ml)	salt
¼ tsp (1 ml)	black pepper

In a bowl, with an electric mixer, beat together the whipping cream and the butter until creamy. Add the Parmesan cheese and beat until smooth. Set aside.

Place the asparagus pieces in a steamer basket over boiling water and steam for 3 to 5 minutes—just until the asparagus turns bright green. Remove from heat and dump into a bowl of cold water to stop the asparagus from cooking any further. Drain and set aside.

Heat the olive oil in a large skillet over medium heat. Add the green onion and stir for 2 minutes, then toss in the asparagus and let cook for just a minute more, until heated through. Remove from heat.

Cook the fettuccine in a large pot of boiling salted water. Drain it thoroughly and dump it back into the pot you cooked it in (no heat!). Add the Parmesan cheese/butter mixture by spoonfuls, stirring until melted into a creamy sauce. Chuck in the asparagus, salt and pepper, and toss well until fettuccine is coated with the sauce. Serve immediately. Try not to swoon.

Makes 4 incredible servings.

Classic Spaghetti with Meatballs DF

A red-and-white checkered tablecloth. A wine bottle with a candle stuck in it. A basket of garlic bread. Spaghetti and meatballs. A *Lady and the Tramp* classic.

2 tbsp (30 ml)	olive oil or vegetable oil
½	medium onion, chopped
2 cloves	garlic, squished
½	medium sweet green pepper, chopped
½ cup (125 ml)	sliced mushrooms
3 cups (750 ml)	spaghetti sauce (homemade [see page 111] if you have it, or use a 28 oz/796 ml can or jar of prepared sauce)
½ tsp (2 ml)	dried oregano
½ tsp (2 ml)	dried basil
1 batch	Plain Old Meatballs, browned (see recipe on page 74)
	Salt and pepper if needed
	Parmesan cheese for sprinkling if desired

In a large skillet or Dutch oven, heat the oil over medium heat. Add the onion and garlic, and cook, stirring, for 3 to 5 minutes—until just beginning to soften. Now add the green pepper and sliced mushrooms, and cook for another 3 to 5 minutes. Add the spaghetti sauce, oregano and basil, and bring to a simmer.

Plunk the Plain Old Meatballs into the simmering sauce. Cover and cook, stirring occasionally, for 20 to 30 minutes, or until the flavors are blended and the meatballs are tender.

Serve over freshly cooked spaghetti, sprinkled with grated Parmesan cheese.

Makes about 4 servings.

Spaghetti Carbonara

This pasta dish cooks in the time it takes to boil the spaghetti. No one will believe it when they find out how you made it. Maybe you shouldn't tell them.

½ lb (250 g)	uncooked spaghetti
6 slices	bacon, chopped into little pieces
2	eggs, beaten
½ cup (125 ml)	grated Parmesan cheese
½ tsp (2 ml)	red pepper flakes (optional—but good)
	Salt and black pepper to taste

Put a large pot of salted water on high heat and bring to a boil.

While the water is heating, chop the bacon and have it ready. Beat the eggs with the Parmesan cheese in a large bowl and set aside. This dish comes together quickly, and you won't have time to mess around once you begin cooking.

When the water boils, stir in the spaghetti.

While the spaghetti is cooking, place a small skillet over medium heat. Add the bacon and red pepper flakes, and cook, stirring often, until the bacon is crisp but not incinerated. Tip the skillet gently and pour all but about 2 tbsp (30 ml) of the bacon fat into an empty container (not down the drain!). Set the skillet with the bacon and reserved fat aside for a moment.

When the spaghetti is done scoop out about ½ cup (125 ml) of the spaghetti water (you'll need it in a minute), then drain the pasta well, but don't rinse it. Dump it into the bowl with the eggs and Parmesan cheese. Add the bacon and the reserved fat and toss well, adding just enough of the reserved cooking water to make the sauce creamy. The heat of the spaghetti actually cooks the eggs, and the whole thing combines into a delicious sauce you'd never in a million years guess was made in about a minute. Season with salt and pepper if needed and serve right away—pronto.

This recipe makes only 2 servings, but you can double it to serve more people.

Perfect Pesto Sauce EF

Pesto sauce is a summer miracle. Make it when you can get really good fresh basil leaves. It freezes really well, so make extra and pack it into small containers to put away for the winter. Recipe can be doubled.

½ cup (125 ml)	olive oil
¼ cup (50 ml)	pine nuts (or substitute almonds or walnuts if you must)
2 cups (500 ml)	fresh basil leaves, rinsed, dried and firmly packed into the measuring cup
2 cloves	garlic (or more if you're that type of person)
½ tsp (2 ml)	salt
¾ cup (175 ml)	grated Parmesan cheese (*freshly* grated if possible)

Heat 1 tbsp (15 ml) of the olive oil in a small skillet over low heat. Add the pine nuts (or whatever nuts you're using) and toast *very gently*, stirring constantly for about 3 minutes, until the nuts are lightly browned. Watch this like a hawk because you don't want to burn them. (Pine nuts are crazy expensive.) Set aside to cool.

Cram the basil leaves, pine nuts, garlic, salt and the remaining olive oil into the container of a food processor or a blender. Blend until almost smooth, scraping the sides down several times so that the mixture blends evenly. A little texture is okay—but no big leafy clumps, please. Add the Parmesan cheese and blend briefly just to mix.

To serve, spoon your Perfect Pesto Sauce into hot, freshly cooked pasta—any shape—and toss well until evenly coated. If the mixture seems a bit dry, you can add a little of the pasta cooking water to it to thin it. Transfer to a serving bowl and serve immediately.

Makes enough sauce for 4 servings of pasta.

Single-Skillet Spaghetti EF

How can you not love a recipe that leaves you with nothing more than a spoon and single frying pan to wash?

1 lb (500 g)	lean ground beef, ground turkey or ground chicken
2 cups (500 ml)	sliced mushrooms
1	medium onion, chopped
1	medium sweet green pepper, chopped
1 can (28 oz/796 ml)	diced tomatoes
1 cup (250 ml)	water
1½ cups (375 ml)	broken uncooked spaghetti
1 tsp (5 ml)	oregano
1 tsp (5 ml)	salt
¼ tsp (1 ml)	black pepper
2 cups (500 ml)	shredded cheese (mozzarella, cheddar or whatever)

In a large skillet, combine the ground meat, mushrooms, onions, and green pepper. Cook over medium-high heat until the meat is browned and the vegetables are softened—10 to 12 minutes.

Dump in the tomatoes, water, broken uncooked spaghetti, oregano, salt and pepper. Bring to a boil, then reduce the heat to medium low. Cover, and cook for 15 to 20 minutes, stirring occasionally, or until the spaghetti is tender. Remove from heat, stir in the cheese and serve.

Makes about 4 servings.

Lasagna to Die For

The genius who invented oven-ready lasagna noodles deserves a medal. Eliminating the annoying noodle-boiling step was a great leap forward in lasagna evolution. If you can make the Bolognese Sauce ahead of time, you can throw together this lasagna in nothing flat.

1 recipe	Bolognese Sauce (see page 116)
2 cups (500 ml)	ricotta or cottage cheese
2	eggs
2 tbsp (30 ml)	chopped fresh parsley (if you have it)
3 cups (750 ml)	grated mozzarella cheese
¼ cup (50 ml)	grated Parmesan cheese
15	oven-ready lasagna noodles

Preheat the oven to 350°F (180°C). Grease a 9 x 13-inch (23 x 33 cm) rectangular baking dish.

In a small bowl, mix the ricotta or cottage cheese, eggs and parsley.

Spread about 1 cup (250 ml) of the Bolognese Sauce on the bottom of the prepared baking dish—it won't quite cover the bottom, but that's okay. Arrange 5 of the lasagna noodles on the sauce, covering the entire bottom of the baking dish, with just a bit of space between the noodles. (You may need to slice one of the noodles so that the whole business fits together right.) Spread 2 cups (500 ml) of Bolognese Sauce over the noodles, then spoon half the ricotta mixture over the sauce (dollop it on as evenly as you can). Sprinkle with 1 cup (250 ml) of the mozzarella cheese. Repeat: 5 more noodles, 2 cups (500 ml) of sauce, the rest of the ricotta and another cup (250 ml) of mozzarella. Are you still with me?

Finally, put the last 5 lasagna noodles on top, spread the rest of the sauce over them, then sprinkle with the remaining mozzarella and all the Parmesan cheese. Whew!

Cover the baking dish loosely with foil (try not to let the foil touch the cheese) and bake for 30 minutes. Remove the foil and bake for another 15 minutes, or until the sauce is bubbling and the lasagna noodles are tender (poke a knife into the middle to make sure).

Makes 8-ish servings.

Vegetarian alert

Yes! You too can make Lasagna to Die For. Substitute a chunky vegetarian pasta sauce for the Bolognese Sauce in the preceding recipe. Sauté 1 cup (250 ml) each chopped mushrooms and diced zucchini in a bit of olive oil until tender. Add to 4 cups (1 l) meatless spaghetti sauce (homemade or store-bought) along with 2 cups (500 ml) raw chopped fresh spinach. Otherwise, follow the lasagna recipe.

Macaroni and Cheese Not from a Box EF

Yes, there are times when you want macaroni and cheese from a box—neon orange, artificially flavored and very fast. But then there are times when you want the other kind. The kind with lots of real cheese and a crunchy top—the kind that takes more than seven minutes to make. This is it. And it is good.

3 cups (750 ml)	uncooked elbow macaroni (or other medium-size pasta)
1 *double* recipe	Basic White Sauce (see page 126)
3 cups (750 ml)	grated sharp cheddar cheese
1 cup (250 ml)	fresh bread crumbs
2 tbsp (30 ml)	butter, melted
½ tsp (2 ml)	salt
	Black pepper to taste

Preheat the oven to 350°F (180°C). Grease a 2- or 3-quart (2 or 3 l) ovenproof baking casserole, any shape. (Pour water into a baking dish with a measuring cup to figure out how much it will hold.)

Cook the macaroni in a large pot of boiling salted water until tender. Drain thoroughly and rinse with cold water to stop any further cooking. Return the cooked macaroni to the pot—but don't put the pot back on the heat. Set aside.

While the macaroni is cooking, make a *double* recipe of white sauce (this means you should *double* the amounts of all the ingredients). Remove the saucepan with the white sauce from the heat and stir in grated cheese, mixing until the cheese is completely melted and the sauce is smooth. Taste, and add salt and pepper if you think the sauce needs it. Add the cheese sauce to the macaroni and stir until mixed. Transfer to the prepared casserole.

Mix the bread crumbs with the melted butter and sprinkle this on top of the macaroni. Place in the preheated oven and bake for 30 to 40 minutes, or until the sauce is bubbly and the topping is crisp and golden. You can, if you must, eat this with ketchup.

Makes 4 to 6 servings.

Basic White Sauce EF

Everyone should know how to make a basic white sauce. You will get endless mileage out of this recipe—memorize it and you will look like a Food Network star. You can add some chopped fresh herbs to this, or garlic, or grated cheese to make it into cheese sauce.

2 tbsp (30 ml)	butter
2 tbsp (30 ml)	all-purpose flour
1 cup (250 ml)	milk
½ tsp (2 ml)	salt
	Black pepper to taste

Melt the butter in a small saucepan over medium heat. Stir in the flour, mixing well. Cook very gently for a minute or two, stirring constantly. Now very slowly stir in the milk. At first the mixture will be lumpy, but as you stir it over the heat, it will become smooth, begin to thicken, and come to a boil. Continue cooking the sauce over low heat for 3 to 5 minutes more, stirring constantly so that it doesn't stick to the bottom of the saucepan and burn.

Season with salt and pepper if you think the sauce needs it. If you're using herbs, add them now. If you want to add cheese, remove the pot from heat and stir in the cheese (about ½ cup/125 ml), mixing until the sauce is smooth and the cheese is melted. Don't cook the sauce after you've added the cheese—it may become stringy.

Makes about 1 cup (250 ml) of white sauce.

Extraordinary Eggs

Outrageous Omelets GF

An omelet is nothing more than a scrambled egg pancake with a filling. The trick is to cook the egg so it isn't rubbery and then to get it out of the pan in one piece. No big deal once you have the hang of it. And even your failures can be served as scrambled eggs. If you happen to have a nonstick skillet, this is the perfect use for it.

3	eggs
1 tbsp (15 ml)	water
1 tbsp (15 ml)	butter
	Salt and black pepper to taste
	Outrageous filling (see left for ideas)

In a small bowl, beat the eggs with the water until the white and yolk are well mixed.

In a 10-inch (25 cm) skillet, heat the butter over medium heat until it begins to get foamy—don't let it brown. Pour the eggs into the pan, reduce the heat slightly to medium low and let them cook, undisturbed, for just 1 minute. As the omelet begins to set underneath, gently lift the edges with a spatula and allow uncooked egg to run under the cooked part. Keep doing this until the omelet is mostly set but still moist on top. (This takes a bit of practice to get just right. Don't panic—it'll be fine.)

Sprinkle the top of the omelet with salt and pepper, and spoon your already prepared outrageous filling onto one half of the uncooked side of the omelet. Gently fold the unfilled half over the filled half and let the omelet continue to cook for just a moment or two to melt any cheese and heat the filling. Now carefully slide the whole thing onto a plate and serve immediately. If the omelet sticks to the skillet—this can happen if you're not using a nonstick pan—carefully slide a spatula under the omelet to loosen it before sliding it out. If it's really stuck, you can always just lift it out of the pan with a pancake turner thingy—not as cool a move, but the omelet is still delicious.

Voilà! An Outrageous Omelet for 1.

Outrageous Omelet Fillings

- Diced cooked potato (leftover is fine) sautéed with onion and chopped bacon
- Chopped ham and Swiss cheese
- Spaghetti sauce, chopped pepperoni and mozzarella cheese (pizza omelet!)
- Mushrooms sautéed with onions
- Salsa, canned black beans and Monterey Jack cheese (taco omelet!)
- Sautéed green pepper, onion and tomato with cheddar cheese
- Diced apples sautéed in butter with cinnamon and sugar

Unfettered Frittatas GF

A frittata is an omelet, only easier. You make it with the same ingredients, but it doesn't require any finicky messing around or fancy folding while it cooks.

¼ cup (50 ml)	olive oil or vegetable oil
1	medium onion, chopped
1½ cups (375 ml)	any sliced or diced vegetable, raw or cooked (mushrooms, zucchini, green beans, peppers, potato, spinach—*anything*)
6	eggs, beaten
¼ cup (50 ml)	grated Parmesan cheese, divided
½ tsp (2 ml)	salt
¼ tsp (1 ml)	black pepper
	Additional herbs or spices—whatever makes sense
2 tbsp (30 ml)	butter

Heat the oil in a 10-inch (25 cm) skillet—nonstick if you have one. Add the sliced onion and sauté for about 5 minutes, until softened. Throw in whatever vegetables you're using and cook them with the onion, stirring occasionally. Raw vegetables will obviously require more cooking than those already cooked—so pay attention. Sauté raw veggies until they're tender. Just stir the cooked ones around a bit.

Remove the pan from heat. Transfer the onion vegetable mixture to a medium-size bowl and let cool for a couple of minutes. Add the beaten eggs, half the Parmesan cheese, the salt, pepper and whatever herbs or spices you're using. Stir to mix.

Over medium heat, melt the butter in the same skillet you cooked the onion and other vegetables in. When the butter begins to get foamy, pour in the mixture of eggs and vegetables, turn down the heat to low and cook the frittata, uncovered, for 15 to 20 minutes, or just until the eggs are set. They'll still be a little wet and wobbly in the middle—that's okay.

Preheat the broiler element of your oven and adjust the top rack to the highest possible position. Sprinkle the top of the frittata with the remaining Parmesan cheese, then slide the pan under the broiler for about a minute or two—just until the top is set and lightly browned. *Very* lightly browned.

Loosen the edges of the frittata by running a knife around the pan, then slide the frittata out onto a serving plate and cut into wedges to serve.

Makes 3 or 4 servings.

Quirky Quiches

Fancy French cousin to the Italian frittata, with a certain Omelet Family resemblance. If you use a frozen, ready-to-bake pastry shell, you can throw a quiche together in about 15 minutes. If you want to make your own pastry (see page 170), it'll take a little longer.

1	9-inch (23 cm) unbaked pastry crust, store-bought or homemade
2 tbsp (30 ml)	butter, olive oil or vegetable oil
½ cup (125 ml)	chopped onion
1½ cups (375 ml)	any sliced or diced vegetable, raw or cooked (mushrooms, zucchini, green beans, peppers, potato, spinach—*anything*)
2 cups (500 ml)	shredded cheese (Swiss, cheddar, Monterey Jack— any kind except the processed cheese slice kind)
3	eggs
1 cup (250 ml)	milk or plain yogurt
½ tsp (2 ml)	salt
¼ tsp (1 ml)	black pepper
	Additional herbs or spices—to suit the occasion

Preheat the oven to 375°F (190°C).

First, get your crust ready. If you're using a store-bought pastry crust, defrost it according to the directions on the package. If you're using your own homemade pastry, roll it out and crimp the edges so it will look all pretty and pie-crusty. Set aside.

Heat the butter or oil in a large skillet over medium heat. Add the onion, and sauté, stirring, for about 5 minutes, or until softened. Add the sliced or diced vegetables and cook for a few minutes. If you're using raw vegetables, cook them just until they're softened. If you're using precooked vegetables, they'll just need to be sautéed for a minute or two to wake them up a bit. Let this mixture cool for a couple of minutes, then spread it in the bottom of the pie crust. Sprinkle the shredded cheese evenly over the vegetables.

In a small bowl, beat the eggs together with the milk or yogurt, the salt, pepper and anything else that might fit your mood (oregano? paprika? cayenne? basil?). Pour over the cheese and vegetables.

Bake in the preheated oven for 35 to 40 minutes, until puffed and golden and a knife poked into the middle comes out cleanish.

Makes about 4 servings.

Scrambled Pepper Eggs GF

A sad lonely pepper, a single leftover potato, a few eggs. Toast a couple of bagels or nuke some tortillas. Dinner for two. In 15 minutes.

1 tbsp (15 ml)	butter
½	medium onion, chopped
1	medium green peppers, diced (jalapeño, anyone?)
1	cooked potato, peeled and diced
4	eggs
½ tsp (2 ml)	salt
¼ tsp (1 ml)	pepper
	Salsa and cheese for a Mexican spin

Melt half the butter in a medium skillet over medium heat. Add the onion and peppers, and sauté for 6 to 8 minutes, until softened. Add the potato and continue cooking for another 5 minutes, stirring often. Dump into a bowl.

Beat the eggs with the salt and pepper. Melt the remaining butter in the skillet over medium heat. Pour in the eggs and cook, stirring constantly, until almost set—about 2 minutes. Stir in the vegetable mixture and serve immediately with toasted bagels or wrapped in a warm tortilla with some salsa and shredded cheese.

Makes 2 servings.

Five Easy Ways to Turn Eggs into Dinner

Scrambled Eggs, Ham and Cheese Panini
Fill a soft panini roll with scrambled eggs, sliced ham or prosciutto and cheese. Toast on both sides in a sandwich grill or frying pan, pressing to flatten.

Egg Fried Rice
Prepare Fried Rice with Whatever (see page 106), but use scrambled eggs instead of any meat, fish or chicken.

Egg-Drop Ramen Noodles
Stir a beaten egg into your favorite ramen noodles. Let cook, stirring, until the egg sets in ribbons and you're done.

Scrambled Macaroni
Scramble an egg or two with onion and garlic, toss in a handful of yesterday's leftover pasta and cook until heated through. Sprinkle with cheese.

Eggs in Your Salad
Chop up a hard-boiled egg or two and toss with your green salad. Add some crumbled bacon bits, if you want, and serve with fresh crusty bread.

Cheese and Bread Strata

Best. Brunch. Dish. Ever. Assemble it the day before you want to serve it, and in the morning it magically bakes without you having to lift a finger (except to turn on the oven). You'll look like a genius. Just smile and say you're welcome.

16	slices of bread, any kind—fresh, stale, whatever.
4 cups (1 l)	shredded cheese, any kind (a mixture is fine)
4	green onions, chopped
5	eggs, beaten
3 cups (750 ml)	milk
1 tbsp (15 ml)	prepared mustard (Dijon if you have it)
1 tsp (5 ml)	salt
¼ tsp (1 ml)	ground cayenne pepper
1 or 2	medium tomatoes, sliced
⅓ cup (75 ml)	grated Parmesan cheese

Grease a 9 x 13-inch (23 x 33 cm) rectangular baking dish.

Line the prepared baking dish with a layer of bread slices. You may need to cut them up a bit so they cover the bottom, jigsaw puzzle style. Don't obsess over this—just do the best you can. Sprinkle bread layer with one-third of the cheese and one-third of the green onions. Repeat two more times: bread, cheese, onions, bread, cheese, onions—making a total of 3 layers of each, ending with green onions. If you're including any of the optional ingredients (suggestions below) just add them between the layers.

In a bowl, beat the eggs with the milk, mustard, salt and cayenne. Pour over the layers in the baking dish, cover the whole thing with foil or plastic wrap and refrigerate overnight. Or longer. Even a couple of days in the fridge is okay.

When you're ready to bake, preheat the oven to 350°F (180°C).

Unwrap the baking dish, arrange the tomato slices artistically on top and sprinkle with Parmesan cheese. Place in the oven and bake for 50 to 60 minutes, or until puffed in the middle and lightly browned. If you poke a knife into the center of the strata, it should come out clean.

Makes 4 to 6 servings.

Optional additions (choose one or more)

- browned sausage meat
- raw baby spinach leaves
- sautéed hot or sweet peppers
- sautéed mushrooms
- chopped cooked bacon
- sautéed zucchini slices

Middle Eastern Shakshuka GF

Is it a dance? A disease? A small furry animal? None of the above. It's a ridiculously easy concoction of eggs poached in a tasty tomato sauce—excellent for brunch, perfect for dinner, good enough for company.

2 tbsp (30 ml)	olive oil or vegetable oil
1	medium onion, chopped
1	jalapeño pepper (optional—if you want a little heat)
2 cloves	garlic, minced or pressed
2 tsp (10 ml)	paprika
½ tsp (2 ml)	cumin
2 cups (500 ml)	diced tomatoes, fresh or canned
⅓ cup (75 ml)	water
½ tsp (2 ml)	salt
¼ tsp (1 ml)	black pepper
4	eggs
½ cup (125 ml)	crumbled feta cheese
¼ cup (50 ml)	chopped cilantro or fresh parsley

Heat the oil in a 10-inch (25 cm) skillet over medium heat. Add the onions and jalapeño pepper and cook, stirring, for about 5 minutes, or until softened. Add the garlic, paprika and cumin, and continue cooking for about 2 minutes. Stir in the tomatoes, water, salt and pepper, and cook, stirring often, until the sauce begins to thicken—about 10 minutes.

Crack one of the eggs into a small bowl—be careful not to break the yolk. With a spoon, make an indentation in the simmering sauce—this doesn't have to be perfect—and gently drop the egg into the little hollow. Repeat with the remaining eggs. Try to keep them as far apart from one another in the pan as possible so that they don't fuse. Cover the pan with a lid, and cook for 5 or 6 minutes—basting the eggs once or twice with the sauce—until they're set but the yolks are still runny.

Sprinkle the feta cheese and cilantro or parsley overtop the whole mess, cover pan for 1 minute—no more than that—and serve.

This goes well with warmed pita bread or a crusty baguette to soak up all that delicious sauce.

Makes 2 servings—but you can easily double it to serve 4 if you have a very large skillet.

Something Fishy

Frozen or fresh? Although you would think that fresh fish is, well, fresher, this may not be the case. Fish that has been flash-frozen at the source is often fresher than fish that's been shipped across the country (or across the world). Properly cooked, you probably couldn't tell the difference.

Fish à la Foil GF EF

The ultimate convenience food. This cooks in minutes, and if you eat it right out of the foil, no dishes to wash.

¼ cup (50 ml)	butter, melted
2 tbsp (30 ml)	chopped parsley
1 tbsp (15 ml)	lemon juice
1½ lb (750 g)	fish fillets, defrosted if frozen
1 tsp (5 ml)	salt
¼ tsp (1 ml)	black pepper
2	medium carrots, coarsely grated
1	small onion, chopped
1 cup (250 ml)	shredded Swiss or cheddar cheese

Preheat the oven to 450°F (230°C). Have ready four 12-inch (30 cm) squares of heavy-duty aluminum foil and grease them lightly.

In a small bowl, combine the butter, parsley and lemon juice. In another bowl, combine the carrots, onion and cheese.

On each square of foil, spread some of the parsley mixture, dividing it evenly among the 4 portions. Top each with 1 serving of fish (again, divide the fish evenly among the 4 squares) and sprinkle with salt and pepper. Now top the fish with the vegetable and cheese mixture. Fold the foil into packets, forming a tight seal on top and at the sides.

Place the packets on a baking sheet and bake in the preheated oven for 20 to 25 minutes.

Remove packets from the oven, place 1 packet on each plate and allow each eater to peel open their own. Surprise!

Makes 4 servings.

Crispy Potato Chip Fish

Absolutely juvenile! Totally unsophisticated! Very crunchy and delicious.

½ cup (125 ml)	Creamy Italian Dressing (see recipe on page 36 or use store-bought)
1½ lbs (750 ml)	fish fillets
3 cups (375 ml)	potato chips
1 cup (250 ml)	shredded cheddar cheese

Preheat the oven to 400°F (200°C). Grease a cookie sheet.

Pour the salad dressing into a shallow bowl. Dip each fillet into the dressing, turning to coat both sides. Arrange in a single layer on the greased cookie sheet.

Put the potato chips in a large, heavy-duty, zip-top plastic bag and zip it shut, leaving a tiny opening for the air to escape. Now, using a rolling pin, crush the potato chips to smithereens. Sprinkle the crushed chips evenly over the fish on the baking sheet. Top with the shredded cheese. Place in the preheated oven and bake for about 20 minutes, or until the fish flakes when you poke it with a fork.

Makes 4 servings.

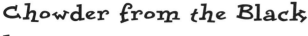

Chowder from the Black Lagoon GF EF

If you're using frozen fish, don't bother thawing it before cooking. Just hack it into chunks and plunk them in the pot. With a salad and some good bread, you've got dinner in less than half an hour.

¼ cup (50 ml)	butter
1	large onion, chopped
3	medium potatoes, peeled and diced
2	medium carrots, grated
2 cups (500 ml)	milk
1 tsp (5 ml)	salt
½ tsp (2 ml)	dried thyme
1 lb (500 g)	fish fillets
2 cups (500 ml)	thickly sliced fresh mushrooms
2 tbsp (30 ml)	chopped fresh parsley

Melt the butter in a large saucepan or Dutch oven over medium heat, then add the onion and cook over medium heat until just softened. Stir in the potatoes, carrots, milk, salt and thyme. Bring to a boil, then turn down the heat to medium low and let simmer for about 15 minutes, or until the potatoes are nearly done.

Cut the fish fillets into 1½-inch (4 cm) chunks and add to the pot along with the mushrooms and the parsley. Stir to mix well, bring to a boil again, reduce heat to medium low and simmer for about 10 minutes, or until the fish is cooked. This makes quite a thick chowder. If you prefer it to be soupier, just add a bit more milk to thin it.

Makes 4 servings.

Maple Glazed Salmon EF DF

Seriously—who can resist this combination? Marinate the fish while you make a salad or cook some potatoes.

⅓ cup (75 ml)	maple syrup
⅓ cup (75 ml)	soy sauce
2 tbsp (30 ml)	cider vinegar
2 cloves	garlic, minced or pressed
1½ lbs (750 g)	salmon fillet, cut into serving pieces

Preheat the oven to 400°F (200°C). Grease a baking dish large enough to hold the salmon fillets in a single layer.

In a small bowl, whisk together the maple syrup, soy sauce, vinegar and garlic. Place the salmon fillets in a shallow dish or zip-top plastic bag. Add the maple marinade and cover the bowl with plastic wrap (or zip the bag shut and press the air out). Refrigerate for at least 30 minutes (but not longer than 1 hour).

Remove the fillets from the marinade and place in the prepared baking dish (discard the marinade). Bake, uncovered, for about 20 minutes, or until the fish flakes when you poke it with a fork.

Makes 4 servings.

Shrimp Factoids

Shells on or shells off? Raw shrimp are sold either with or without their shells. Generally, shell-on shrimp will be less expensive per pound than shelled ones. And the shells help protect the shrimp from drying out in the freezer. But since most recipes ask you to remove the shells before cooking, which kind is a better choice—shell on or shell off? Taking off the shells is not really that much work, so if price is an issue and you're willing to spend a little time, buy shrimp in the shell and peel them yourself. But if you really don't want to be bothered doing all that shell removal, go ahead and buy shelled shrimp.

What about the veins? Often a recipe will tell you to devein shrimp before cooking. Why? No real reason. Removing the black vein that runs along the back of the shrimp is done mostly for appearance. If you don't like the way the vein looks, remove it with a sharp knife before cooking. If you don't care, then just leave it in—it won't kill you.

Shrimp in Garlic Butter GF EF

Let's say you win the lottery. Or some wealthy relative you never met dies and leaves you everything. Or you rob a bank. (No—just kidding—don't do that.) Anyway, let's just suppose you want to splurge. This dish is the way to go.

¼ cup (50 ml)	butter, melted
2 tbsp (30 ml)	olive oil
4 cloves	garlic, minced or pressed
¼ cup (50 ml)	chopped green onions
½ tsp (2 ml)	paprika
½ tsp (2 ml)	hot pepper flakes (optional but good)
½ tsp (2 ml)	salt
¼ tsp (1 ml)	pepper
2 lbs (1 kg)	raw shrimp, as large as you can afford, peeled
2 tbsp (30 ml)	chopped fresh parsley if you have it

Preheat the broiler element of your oven to high. Place the top oven rack as close to the broiler element as possible.

In a large bowl, stir together the butter, oil, garlic, green onions, paprika, hot pepper flakes, salt and pepper. Add the shrimp and toss them until they are completely coated with the butter mixture. Spread the shrimp out on a cookie sheet or shallow baking pan so that they're in a single layer.

Put the pan on the top oven rack and broil for 2 to 3 minutes, then stir, flip the shrimp over, and return them to the oven to broil for another 2 minutes. Sprinkle with parsley and serve immediately—pronto—with crusty bread, tossed with hot cooked pasta or spooned over steamed rice and, of course, a salad.

Makes 4 servings. Less, if you're pigs about it.

Greek Baked Shrimp with Feta GF EF

You can serve this fantastic dish as a main course or as an appetizer. It's almost too good to be so easy.

2 tbsp (30 ml)	olive oil or vegetable oil
1	medium onion, chopped
2 cloves	garlic, minced or pressed
1 cup (250 ml)	chopped green onions
2 cups (500 ml)	diced tomatoes (canned or fresh)
½ cup (125 ml)	chicken or vegetable broth or water
¼ cup (50 ml)	chopped fresh parsley
1 tsp (5 ml)	crumbled dried oregano
1 tsp (5 ml)	salt
¼ tsp (1 ml)	black pepper
2 lbs (1 kg)	raw shrimp, medium or large, shelled
½ cup (125 ml)	crumbled feta cheese

Preheat the oven to 450°F (230°C). Grease a 9- or 10-inch (23 or 25 cm) round or square baking dish.

Heat the oil in a medium skillet over medium heat. Add the onion and cook, stirring, until just starting to soften—about 3 minutes. Add the garlic and green onions and cook, stirring, for 2 minutes, then add the tomatoes, broth or water, parsley, oregano, salt and pepper. Bring to a boil, then reduce the heat to low and simmer, uncovered, for about 15 minutes, or until thickened. (You can spend this time shelling shrimp or making salad. Just a thought.)

Spoon about half the tomato sauce into the prepared baking dish and top with the shrimp. Dollop the remaining tomato sauce over the shrimp and sprinkle evenly with the crumbled feta cheese. Put the baking dish in the oven and bake for 15 to 20 minutes, or until the sauce is bubbling, the shrimp in the center of the dish are pink and the feta cheese is lightly browned.

Serve hot with crusty bread to mop up the delicious sauce.

Makes about 4 servings.

Tunaburgers DF

It's summer and you're surrounded by barbecues. The delicious smell of scorched meat fills the air. All you have in the house is a can of tuna. These burgers are delicious, easy to make and will satisfy that primal need for something charred beyond recognition.

1 can (6.5 oz/184 g)	tuna, drained and flaked
1½ cups (375 ml)	fresh bread crumbs
1	small onion, very finely chopped
1	medium carrot, coarsely grated
1	egg
2 tbsp (30 ml)	mayonnaise
1 tsp (5 ml)	vegetable oil
¼ tsp (2 ml)	salt
¼ tsp (1 ml)	black pepper
	Toasted buns, toppings—the works

In a medium bowl, mix all the ingredients until well mushed. If you have a food processor, now is the time to use it. The tuna mixture must be finely chopped or the burgers may not hold together on the grill. If you don't have a processor, use a fork and mash like crazy. By hand, form the mixture into compact patties.

Place tunaburgers on a preheated barbecue grill and cook over medium-high heat for about 6 to 8 minutes per side, or until golden brown. Serve in a bun with some sliced tomato, mayonnaise and lettuce. Oh, and okay, ketchup too if it'll make you feel more normal.

If you prefer to pan-fry the tunaburgers, heat a little vegetable oil in a large skillet and cook the patties 7 to 10 minutes per side, until golden. You can serve very tiny patties as tuna nuggets with dipping sauce.

Makes 3 to 4 tunaburgers.

Completely Classic Tuna Casserole

Tuna casserole will bring you back to your childhood—turn on the TV, find some good old cartoons and wallow in the moment. Adulthood can wait.

1 cup (250 ml)	uncooked wide noodles
¼ cup (50 ml)	finely chopped onion
1 tbsp (15 ml)	butter
1 can (10 oz/284 ml)	cream of mushroom soup (don't dilute it)
1 can (6.5 oz/184 ml)	tuna, flaked
¾ cup (175 ml)	crushed potato chips

Preheat the oven to 375°F (190°C). Grease a 9-inch (23 cm) round soufflé or casserole dish.

In a saucepan of boiling salted water, cook the noodles until tender. Drain in a colander and rinse under cold running water. Set aside.

Melt the butter in a medium saucepan over medium heat. Add the onions and cook for about 5 minutes, or until softened. Stir in the cooked noodles, mushroom soup and tuna, and mix well. Dump into the prepared casserole dish and sprinkle the top with the crushed potato chips. Bake for 25 to 30 minutes, or until heated through and bubbly.

Feeds 2 or 3 slobs, depending on how big they are.

Vehemently Vegetarian

Going Vegetarian

There are plenty of sensible reasons to go vegetarian, lots of bad ones and quite a few reasons not to even consider it at all. Becoming a vegetarian isn't rocket science, but it does require some understanding of your nutritional needs and an open mind. Oh, and you really do have to like vegetables.

Vegetarian or not, your diet should include foods from each of the following four groups: grain products, vegetables and fruit, milk products and alternatives and meat alternatives. It's total amount of servings from each group at the end of the day that counts—not necessarily each individual meal. So if you're a grazing sort of person who eats all day long, just total everything you eat and make sure it adds up. You could, theoretically, have all your grain servings at breakfast, all your fruit for lunch and everything else for dinner. It would be weird—but you could do it. Or else you can have normal meals with a little from each food group on your plate at the same time. Just like a regular person. Suit yourself.

The food guide on the following page applies to a lacto-ovo vegetarian diet (one that includes eggs and dairy products). Vegans (vegetarians who eat no animal foods whatsoever) have to do a little *extra* homework to be sure they're eating a healthy diet. A doctor or school nutritionist can give you the information you need.

Finally, an active person (who plays sports, dances, runs around like a maniac) will need to eat more of everything than a couch-potato type. Do you fall somewhere in between? Eat what feels right for *you*.

Grain Products (6 to 11 servings per day)

- bread (whole grain is best)
- tortillas
- crackers
- pasta
- rice
- couscous
- barley
- oats
- bulgur wheat
- cornmeal
- cereals—all kinds, hot or cold (minimally sweetened)

Vegetables and Fruit (5 to 9 servings per day)

All fresh, frozen, canned and dried fruits and vegetables, plus things you might not think of, such as:
- spaghetti sauce or salsa
- raisins, dates and other dried fruits
- orange and other fruit juices
- pickles and relishes

Milk Products and Alternatives (2 to 3 servings per day)

- milk
- natural cheese
- yogurt
- sour cream
- cream cheese
- fortified soy, rice or almond milk

Meat Alternatives (2 to 3 servings per day)

- eggs
- beans, peas, lentils
- tofu, tempeh and other soy products
- nuts and seeds (peanuts, almonds, walnuts, sunflower seeds, sesame seeds, pumpkin seeds)
- pretend meat (veggie burgers, veggie dogs, veggie nuggets)

Fats and Sweets (eat sparingly)

Vaguely Chinese Stir-Fry EF DF

The secret to a quick and easy stir-fry is to have every single thing prepared before you start cooking so that you're not madly slicing or measuring in midstir. The prep takes a little time, but the actual cooking is done in minutes. This recipe is infinitely variable—see sidebar for some ideas.

3 tbsp (45 ml)	vegetable oil, divided
2 squares	firm tofu, cut into ½-inch (1 cm) cubes
1 bunch	broccoli, florets cut apart, stems thinly sliced
1	green or red pepper, cut into 1-inch (2 cm) squares
2 cloves	garlic, minced or pressed
4	green onions, halved lengthwise and cut into 1-inch (2 cm) pieces
½ cup (125 ml)	vegetable broth, divided (prepared broth or made from bouillon cubes or powder)
3 tbsp (45 ml)	soy sauce
1 tbsp (15 ml)	cornstarch
1 tsp (5 ml)	sesame oil
¼ cup (50 ml)	cashews or peanuts (cashews really are better)

Arrange all the cut-up vegetables on a large plate, keeping each in its own little pile so that you can add it to the stir-fry separately. Cut up the tofu and have it ready. In a small bowl, stir together ¼ cup of the broth, the soy sauce, cornstarch and sesame oil, then set it aside. Have the garlic minced and the cashews measured. Okay. *Now* you're ready to start cooking.

Pour about half the oil into a wok or large skillet and heat it over high heat. Toss in the tofu pieces and stir-fry until very lightly browned. Transfer the browned tofu from the wok to a bowl and set aside.

Add the rest of the oil to the wok or skillet and heat until a drop of water sizzles when you sprinkle it into the pan. Add the broccoli, pepper and garlic, and stir-fry for 1 or 2 minutes, or until well mixed and glossy with oil. Toss in the green onions, stir, then add the remaining ¼ cup of broth. Slam a cover on the pan and let the vegetables steam for a minute or two, until the broccoli is bright green and starting to become tender. Remove the lid, dump the tofu back into the pan and give it a good stir. Add the soy sauce mixture, stirring constantly. The sauce will thicken and become glossy. Sprinkle the cashews or peanuts over the top and serve immediately, with hot cooked rice or noodles.

Makes 3 or 4 servings.

Variations on a stir-fry (vegetarian and non)

Switch up or add to the veggies, depending on what is available. Snow peas, bean sprouts, thinly sliced carrots, mushrooms, asparagus are all great stir-fry candidates.

Non-vegetarians can add cubed chicken, shelled shrimp or thinly sliced beef or pork instead of or in addition to the tofu.

No tofu? No meat? How about an egg? Scramble an egg or two for a shot of protein.

Leftover pasta—noodles, spaghetti, linguine—are all great in a stir-fry. Add at the end and toss to heat through.

Tofu (oh come on, just try it)

Look, it's not made from pond slime or fish livers or anything weird like that. Tofu is a nice, wholesome food made from perfectly harmless soybeans. It's cheap, packed with protein and low in fat. It doesn't taste like much on its own but absorbs the flavor of whatever it hangs out with. Try it in a few different ways to see what you like.

Bake it!

Buy extra-firm tofu, cut it into sticks or slabs, douse it with barbecue sauce and bake until sizzling. Or cut extra-firm tofu into fingers, dip in beaten egg and bread crumbs and bake on an oiled cookie sheet until crisp (great with ketchup).

Stir-fry it!

Marinate ½-inch (1 cm) cubes of firm tofu in soy sauce before stir-frying with veggies. Throw in a spoonful of Asian chili paste. Amazing!

Freeze it!

Stash a couple of blocks of tofu in the freezer and let them freeze solid, then thaw them out. The texture changes completely. You can now crumble the tofu (as a substitute for ground meat) or slice it into slivers to throw into a stir fry.

Go naked!

The tofu, that is. Just float a few cubes in your soup or toss some into your salad. (Generally recommended for committed tofu converts only.)

Bored?

When you think there's nothing fun left to do in the whole world, when you're feeling overwhelmed by responsibility, when you're just hanging aimlessly around the kitchen—try this. Dump some cornstarch (about a cupful will do) into a bowl. Add water, a bit at a time, and stir. The mixture will be clumpy at first, but as you add drops of water, it begins to loosen up. Suddenly it's a liquid. No, it's a solid. No—*what the heck is this stuff, anyway?* Pick some up with your hand and let it ooze through your fingers. Squeeze it into a ball and it's hard again. Isn't life cool?

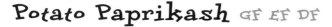

Potato Paprikash GF EF DF

Who says potatoes can't be the main dish? Add a salad and you've got yourself a two-course dinner.

¼ cup (50 ml)	olive oil or vegetable oil
2	medium onions, chopped
6	large potatoes, sliced ¼ inch (.5 cm) thick
1 tbsp (15 ml)	paprika
1 tsp (5 ml)	dried thyme
½ tsp (2 ml)	salt
¼ tsp (1 ml)	black pepper
2 cups (500 ml)	water or vegetable broth
	Sour cream or plain yogurt for serving

Heat the oil in a large skillet over medium heat. Add the onions and sauté for about 5 minutes, or until softened. Add the potatoes and stir them around a little, then sprinkle with the paprika, thyme, salt and pepper. Cook for 2 minutes, then pour in enough water to *almost* (but not quite) cover the potatoes. Slam the lid on the pan, reduce the heat to a medium low and cook for 15 to 20 minutes, or until the potatoes are tender when poked with a fork. Serve with a dollop of sour cream or yogurt if desired.

Makes 2 servings as a main dish, maybe 4 as a side dish.

Alternatives—vegetarian and otherwise

Non-vegetarians can add 2 cups (500 ml) smoked sausage, kielbasa, even hot dogs, cut into 1-inch (2 cm) pieces, to the pan with the onions. This turns the dish into Sausage and Potato Paprikash—a Hungarian classic. Sort of.

Sprinkle the dish with shredded cheese when just about ready to serve. Cover and remove from heat. Let sit just until the cheese is melted.

Toss in a diced block of tofu along with the onions to add a protein component to the dish.

Stuffed Baked Potatoes GF EF

Make more of these than you need, wrap the extras in foil and stash them in the fridge for an excellent midnight snack. More satisfying than a bag of chips and better for you.

4	large potatoes
½ cup (125 ml)	cottage cheese
¼ cup (50 ml)	grated cheddar cheese
¼ cup (50 ml)	butter
½ tsp (2 ml)	salt
1¼ tsp (1 ml)	black pepper

Preheat the oven to 400°F (200°C).

Scrub the potatoes, poke a few fork holes into each one (to prevent explosion) and bake directly on the rack of the preheated oven until *really* done—45 minutes to 1 hour.

Alternatively, you can bake the potatoes in a microwave. Poke holes in the potatoes and arrange in a circle on a paper towel. Zap them on high power for 12 to 15 minutes (timing depends on your oven and the size of the potatoes). About halfway through the baking time, flip the potatoes end to end and over to make sure they cook evenly.

Cut a lengthwise slice from the top of each potato and scoop the insides into a bowl. Mash the potato pulp with the cottage cheese, the cheddar cheese, the butter, salt and pepper.

Spoon the mixture back into the shells, mounding the filling attractively (there will be more filling than was originally in the potato). You can leave them au naturel or sprinkle the tops with a little paprika to be extra cheerful. Place on a baking sheet (if you're baking them right away), or wrap in foil and refrigerate or freeze for future consumption.

About 15 minutes before you want to eat, unwrap the stuffed potatoes and bake them at 400°F (200°C) until heated through and very lightly browned.

Serves 4 as a side dish or snack, fewer as a main course.

Potato and Pea Curry GF EF DF

Add a bowl of chutney, some sliced cucumbers and some warm flatbread, and your karma will thank you.

6	medium potatoes, whole—don't peel
¼ cup (50 ml)	vegetable oil
1 tsp (5 ml)	whole mustard seeds
2	onions, chopped
1 tbsp (15 ml)	curry powder
¼ tsp (1 ml)	cayenne pepper (or as much as you like)
1 cup (250 ml)	frozen peas
1 tsp (5 ml)	salt
1 cup (250 ml)	water
¼ cup (50 ml)	chopped cilantro (if you have it) or fresh parsley

Cook the potatoes in boiling water until tender but still a little firm in the middle. Drain, let cool for a couple of minutes, then peel them (they should practically peel themselves) and cut into ½-inch (1 cm) cubes. (Cooking potatoes with the peels on helps prevent them from getting waterlogged.) Set aside.

Heat the oil in a large skillet over medium heat. Add the mustard seeds. Enjoy the show as they crackle and pop in the pan, then when the popping dies down add the onions. Cook, stirring, for 7 to 10 minutes, or until the onions start to brown. Add the curry powder and cayenne, stir for a couple of minutes and then add the potatoes, peas, salt and water. Reduce the heat to low, cover the skillet and cook curry for about 5 minutes. Sprinkle with the cilantro and cook for another 10 minutes, adding a bit more water if the curry becomes dry.

Makes 2 or 3 servings.

Variations on a curry

Try this with canned chickpeas (1 cup/250 ml), drained and rinsed, instead of the green peas.

Instead of potatoes, substitute a large head of cauliflower (or two small ones) broken up into florets. Add the florets, uncooked, to the onion mixture in the pan, then follow the recipe as above. Cook until cauliflower is tender.

Eggplant Parmigiana

Every vegetarian needs a few recipes to haul out when carnivores (your parents?) come to dinner. This is a good one. So delicious and satisfying that no one will care there's no meat.

½ cup (125 ml)	olive oil or vegetable oil
2	eggs
½ cup (125 ml)	milk
2 cups (500 ml)	dry bread crumbs
½ tsp (2 ml)	oregano
½ tsp (2 ml)	salt
¼ tsp (1 ml)	black pepper
2	medium eggplants
4 cups (1 l)	spaghetti sauce (homemade [see page 111] if you have it, or prepared sauce from a jar or can)
½	cup (125 ml) grated Parmesan cheese
3 cups (750 ml)	shredded mozzarella cheese

Preheat the broiler element of your oven. Brush a cookie sheet generously with some of the oil. Grease a 9 x 13-inch (23 x 33 cm) rectangular baking dish.

In a small dish, beat the eggs with the milk. In another dish, combine the bread crumbs, oregano, salt and pepper.

Without peeling them, slice the eggplants crosswise into ¼-inch (.5 cm) rounds. Working with 1 slice at a time, dip first into the egg mixture, then into the bread crumbs, turning to coat both sides. When all the slices are breaded, arrange as many as will fit in a single layer on the prepared cookie sheet. (You'll need to do 2 or 3 batches—don't crowd.) Broil for 3 to 4 minutes, then flip the slices and broil for another 3 to 4 minutes. The eggplant should be lightly browned on both sides and tender when poked with a fork. Remove the slices from the baking sheet and set aside. Brush cookie sheet with a bit more oil and repeat until you've done all the eggplant slices. You may not need to use the entire ½ cup (125 ml) of the oil.

Turn off the broiler and preheat the oven to 350°F (180°C).

Spread ½ cup (125 ml) of the spaghetti sauce on the bottom of the prepared baking dish (just a thin layer). On this, arrange a layer of eggplant slices, cutting them, if necessary, to cover the bottom. Spread with 1 cup (250 ml) of spaghetti sauce, a sprinkle of Parmesan cheese and 1 cup (250 ml) of mozzarella cheese. Repeat—another layer of eggplant slices, another cup of spaghetti sauce, a sprinkle of Parmesan and a cup of mozzarella. Finish with the rest of the eggplant slices, the rest of the spaghetti sauce and the rest of the Parmesan cheese. You'll have some mozzarella left—good, you'll need it later.

Bake in the preheated oven for 30 minutes. Sprinkle on the remaining mozzarella cheese and bake for another 15 minutes, or until bubbling and the cheese is melted.

Makes 6 to 8 servings.

Welsh Rabbit

Relax—no actual bunnies in this recipe. Welsh Rabbit is just a funny name for melted cheese on toast.

2 tbsp (30 ml)	butter
½ cup (125 ml)	beer (leftover flat beer is fine)
1	egg
2 tsp (10 ml)	mustard
1 tsp (5 ml)	Worcestershire sauce
3 cups (750 ml)	grated sharp cheddar cheese
2	tomatoes, sliced
	Toasted English muffins, or toasted French bread, or pretty much toasted anything

In a small saucepan, melt the butter over low heat. Whisk together the beer, egg, mustard and Worcestershire sauce. Add to the butter along with the cheese. Cook this mixture, stirring or whisking constantly, until smooth and thickened—about 8 to 10 minutes.

On each plate, arrange two toasted English muffin halves (or whatever toast you're using) and top each one with a slice of tomato. Spoon the cheese sauce over everything and serve immediately.

Makes 3 or 4 servings.

Chunky Vegetable Stew

Here's a substantial vegetarian stew that will warm your innards on a chilly evening. This is great spooned over rice, couscous, quinoa or pasta.

2 tbsp (30 ml)	olive oil or vegetable oil
2	medium onions, cut into large chunks
2 cups (500 ml)	cauliflower florets
2 cups (500 ml)	potatoes cut into 1-inch/2 cm cubes
1	large sweet potato, peeled and cut into 1-inch/ 2 cm chunks
2 cups (500 ml)	fresh mushrooms, halved or quartered
4 cloves	garlic, minced or pressed
1½ cups (375 ml)	diced tomatoes (canned or fresh)
1½ cups (375 ml)	vegetable broth (prepared broth or made from bouillon cubes or powder)
1 can (19 oz/540 ml)	lentils, drained and rinsed
½ tsp (2 ml)	hot red pepper flakes
1 tsp (5 ml)	salt
¼ tsp (1 ml)	black pepper
2 cups (500 ml)	coarsely chopped fresh spinach leaves

Heat the oil in a large pot or Dutch oven over medium heat. Add the onion and cook, stirring, for 2 or 3 minutes, until the onion begins to soften. Add the cauliflower, sweet potato and regular potato, and cook for about 10 minutes, stirring occasionally. Add the mushrooms and garlic, and cook for 5 minutes. Add the tomatoes, vegetable broth, lentils, salt, hot pepper flakes and black pepper, and bring to a boil. Cover the pot with a lid, reduce the heat to medium low and continue to cook for about 20 minutes, or until all the vegetables are tender. Toss in the spinach leaves, cover and cook for a minute or two more, and serve.

Makes 4 to 6 servings.

Meatless Chili GF EF

Years ago, when great herds of wild eggplants roamed the prairies, frontier cooks invented this chili to make use of the seemingly endless supply. Alas, those days are over. But even though we now get our eggplants from a store, we can still make this chili.

1	large eggplant, cut into ½-inch (1 cm) cubes
1 tsp (5 ml)	salt
¼ cup (50 ml)	olive oil or vegetable oil
2	onions, chopped
2	medium zucchini, cut in ½-inch (1 cm) cubes
2	red or green peppers (or one of each), chopped
4 cloves	garlic, minced or pressed
1 can (28 oz/796 ml)	diced tomatoes
3 tbsp (45 ml)	Mexican chili powder
1 tbsp (15 ml)	cumin
1 tsp (5 ml)	dried oregano
½ tsp (2 ml)	hot pepper flakes (or more, or less)
1 can (19 oz/540 ml)	red kidney beans, drained and rinsed
1½ cups (375 ml)	frozen or canned corn niblets
	Salt and black pepper if needed
	Shredded cheese, sour cream, chopped jalapeño peppers for serving

Place the eggplant cubes in a colander or strainer set over a bowl and sprinkle with the salt. Toss to coat, then let drain for an hour or so. Pat the cubes dry with paper towel and discard the liquid that has seeped out. (Salting removes some of the excess water from the eggplant so that it cooks faster and doesn't absorb as much oil, but if you're in a big hurry, you can skip this step.)

Heat the oil in a large saucepan or Dutch oven over medium heat. Add the onions, zucchini, peppers and garlic, and cook, stirring, for 5 to 7 minutes, or until vegetables are softened. Add the eggplant cubes and cook for another 5 to 10 minutes, until everything is tender. Dump in the tomatoes, the chili powder, cumin, oregano and hot pepper flakes, and bring to a boil. Reduce the heat to medium low, cover and cook for about 30 minutes, stirring occasionally. Add the beans and the corn, and cook for another 15 minutes. Taste, and adjust the seasoning with salt and pepper if necessary.

Serve over rice, with a glop of sour cream, a sprinkle of grated cheese, some chopped jalapeño peppers—whatever.

Makes about 8 servings.

How to Cook Dried Beans

Sure, you can buy your kidney beans in a can. And there's nothing wrong with them. But, for sheer down and dirty cheapness, nothing beats a bag of good old dried beans. It's not even all that much work.

Measure your beans (any kind) into a saucepan. Look them over and remove all the little alien bits you find—pebbles, specks of dirt, weirdly deformed beans. Cover the beans with cold water, swish them around with your hand and pour the water off. Do it again, just to be sure the beans are well washed—you never know where they've been.

Next, you have to soak them. Add enough fresh cold water to the pan to cover the beans by at least 1½ to 2 inches (4 to 5 cm). Place on the stove, cover and bring to a boil over high heat. Boil for 5 minutes, then turn off the heat and let the beans sit for 1 hour.

To cook, pour off and discard the soaking water. Add enough cold water to fill the pot to at least 1 inch (2 cm) above the beans. You might also add a couple of whole cloves of garlic and a whole peeled onion for extra flavor. Don't add salt. Cover the pot and bring to a boil over medium-high heat. Reduce the heat to medium-low and cook until the beans are soft. Depending on the kind of beans and how fresh they are, this could take anywhere from 30 minutes to 2 hours. Check on them from time to time and add water if necessary so that they're always covered.

Drain the beans, salt them to taste and use them in whatever way you would canned ones. If you have to keep them for a day or two before using, refrigerate the cooked beans in their liquid.

Mostly Moroccan Vegetable Couscous EF DF

Couscous is a tiny grain (a form of pasta, actually) that you can prepare in minutes. It goes deliciously with almost anything you care to spoon onto it—especially a spicy vegetable concoction like this recipe. Exotic but easy.

1 tbsp (15 ml)	olive oil or vegetable oil
1	medium onion, chopped
2 cloves	garlic, minced or pressed
1 cup (250 ml)	vegetable broth (or chicken broth)
1 cup (250 ml)	peeled butternut squash, cut into ½-inch/1 cm cubes
1	medium zucchini, cut into ½-inch/1 cm cubes
1 can (19 oz/540 ml)	chickpeas, drained and rinsed
½ tsp (2 ml)	ground cumin
½ tsp (2 ml)	curry powder
¼ tsp (1 ml)	crushed hot red pepper flakes (or more if you dare)
1 cup (250 ml)	diced tomato (fresh or canned)
¼ cup (50 ml)	raisins
1 tsp (5 ml)	salt
¼ tsp (1 ml)	black pepper
1 cup (250 ml)	dry couscous
1 cup (250 ml)	boiling water

Heat the oil in a large saucepan or Dutch oven over medium heat. Add the onion and garlic, and cook, stirring, until softened—about 5 minutes. Add the broth and the butternut squash, cover, and let the squash simmer until almost tender—about 15 minutes (poke a fork into a squash cube—if it's still firm, cook a little longer).

Add the zucchini, chickpeas, cumin, curry powder and hot pepper flakes, and stir. Replace the cover and let cook for 5 minutes. Now add the tomato, raisins, salt and pepper, and cook for another 5 minutes, or until tomato and raisins are softened and the flavors are blended.

In the meantime, while the vegetables are simmering, prepare the couscous. Place the dry couscous into a bowl or saucepan. Pour the boiling water over it, stir, cover and let sit for 10 minutes. Fluff with a fork and scoop into a serving bowl. That's all there is to it.

Spoon the vegetable mixture over the couscous and serve immediately.

Makes 3 to 4 servings.

Carnivore alert

For a chicken and vegetable couscous, add one or two boneless, skinless chicken breasts, cut into cubes, to the zucchini and chickpeas.

153

Veggie Burgers DF

Oh stop whining. Here's a little veggie-packed something to put on a bun when all your friends are eating hamburgers. Freeze any extras, individually wrapped in plastic or foil, so you'll always be ready for a barbecue.

2 tbsp (30 ml)	olive oil or vegetable oil
2	medium red or green peppers, chopped (or one of each)
3	medium carrots, grated
3	medium potatoes, boiled and mashed (about 2 cups/500ml mashed)
2 cups (500 ml)	coarsely chopped raw spinach, tightly packed to measure
1	large onion, minced or grated
1 cup (250 ml)	bread crumbs
3	eggs, beaten
1 tsp (5 ml)	salt
¼ tsp (1 ml)	black pepper

Heat the oil in a large skillet over medium heat. Add chopped peppers and sauté until soft, about 10 to 12 minutes. Transfer to a large bowl. Add the carrots, mashed potatoes, spinach, onion, bread crumbs, eggs, salt and pepper. Mix well, cover the bowl with plastic wrap and refrigerate for at least 1 hour (or overnight).

To form the patties, scoop out about ½ cup (125 ml) of the mixture and pat into burger-ish shapes, flattening them slightly.

To grill your veggie burgers, brush them on both sides with a little oil, place on a perforated grill-top rack and cook over medium-low heat for about 10 minutes per side, turning them over several times with a spatula to make sure they cook through.

Or you can fry these babies. Heat some oil in a large skillet and cook the veggie burgers over medium heat until golden brown on both sides.

Serve in a bun with the usual array of toppings—ketchup, mustard, mayo, onions, tomatoes, relish, cheese—and so on, and so on.

Makes about 10 veggie burgers.

Baked Stuffed Portobello Mushrooms EF

Portobello mushrooms are the steak of the vegetable world. Fill the large meaty caps with a hearty stuffing and dig in to a very satisfying main dish.

6	large portobello mushroom caps
1 tbsp (15 ml)	olive oil or vegetable oil
1	onion, chopped
2 cloves	garlic, minced or pressed
2 cups (500 ml)	shredded sharp cheddar cheese
1 cup (250 ml)	fresh bread crumbs
¼ cup (50 ml)	chopped fresh parsley or basil
½ tsp (2 ml)	salt
¼ tsp (1 ml)	pepper
	Additional oil for brushing mushrooms

Preheat the oven to 375°F (190°C). Grease a baking dish large enough to hold all the portobello caps without overlapping.

Wipe any dirt off the portobellos or rinse them quickly under running water to clean. Remove the stems by cutting them off where they attach to the caps. Trim off the root end and chop the stems finely. Brush the caps on both sides with a little oil and arrange them, gill-side up, in the prepared baking pan.

Heat the oil in a skillet over medium-high heat. Add the chopped mushroom stems, onion and the garlic, and cook, stirring occasionally, for 6 to 8 minutes, or until the onions are tender. Dump into a large bowl. Add the shredded cheese, bread crumbs, parsley, salt and pepper. Toss to mix.

Spoon the stuffing mixture into the caps, dividing it equally among the mushrooms. Bake in the preheated oven for 20 to 30 minutes, or until the mushrooms are sizzling and the stuffing is hot and lightly browned.

Makes 3 to 4 servings.

Vegetarian Cowboy Beans EF DF

After riding the range all day—roping maverick zucchini, wrangling runaway cabbages, rounding up those herds of wild eggplants—vegetarian cowboys like nothing better than to sit around the old campfire with a heaping plateful of these beans and tell some lies.

1 lb (500 g)	white pea beans or navy beans
4 cups (1 l)	water
2	medium onions, chopped
½ cup (125 ml)	ketchup
¼ cup (50 ml)	brown sugar
¼ cup (50 ml)	maple syrup or molasses
2 tbsp (30 ml)	olive oil or vegetable oil
1 tbsp (15 ml)	vinegar
1 tbsp (15 ml)	prepared mustard
1 tsp (5 ml)	salt
2	tomatoes, thickly sliced

Put the dry beans into a large pot and pick over them carefully, removing any bits that don't look like a bean (pebbles, specks of dirt, that sort of thing). Rinse the beans well, changing the water several times to wash off the dirt. Cover the beans with plenty of fresh water—about an inch or two over the beans—bring to a boil over high heat and cook for 5 minutes. Remove from heat, cover and let the beans soak for 1 hour.

Drain the beans thoroughly—they should have nearly doubled in size—and discard the soaking water. Pour in the 4 cups (1 l) of fresh water, bring to a boil over high heat, then reduce the heat to medium low. Cover them and simmer for 30 minutes.

Preheat the oven to 300°F (150°C).

Drain the beans, but hang on to the cooking liquid. Place the chopped onions in the bottom of an ovenproof Dutch oven or large casserole. Add the drained beans. In a small bowl, mix the ketchup, brown sugar, syrup or molasses, oil, vinegar, mustard and salt. Pour this over the beans, then pour in enough of the reserved cooking liquid so it covers the beans. (If you don't have enough liquid, add some water or vegetable broth.) Arrange the tomato slices over the top, cover tightly and bake in the preheated oven for 5 hours. Really. *Five hours.* (You don't have to sit there watching—go do something useful.)

About halfway through the baking time, lift the lid and give the pot a stir. Replace the cover, and continue baking until the 5 hours are up, adding a little additional liquid if needed to keep the beans just covered. Remove the cover for the last hour of baking to let the beans brown a bit.

Now go sit around the fire, eat your beans and tell some lies. You've put in a long day on the range.

Makes 8 servings.

Bean Burritos EF

Who says you don't have time to make dinner? Here. This will take two minutes.

Burrito supplies

- flour tortillas
- refried beans, homemade (see page 58 for recipe) or canned, heated
- shredded cheddar or Monterey Jack cheese
- salsa
- sour cream
- diced tomatoes
- shredded lettuce
- chopped onion
- chopped jalapeño peppers

Burrito construction

Drop a large blob of warm refried beans onto the middle of your tortilla. Top the beans with any or all of the above ingredients, in whatever order or amount that seems logical.

Now fold the bottom of the tortilla up so that it partly covers the beans and other ingredients.

Next, fold one side in toward the middle, then the other side. Leave the top open.

There. Done.

Pick up the burrito and eat. Or take it with you. Bye.

Baking up a Storm

Basic Homemade Muffins

Even a mediocre homemade muffin, freshly baked and still warm, is so much better than anything you can buy anywhere. Try not to eat them all yourself.

1¾ cup (425 ml)	all-purpose flour
¼ cup (50 ml)	granulated sugar
2½ tsp (12 ml)	baking powder
1	egg, beaten
¾ cup (175 ml)	milk
⅓ cup (75 ml)	vegetable oil or melted butter
1 tsp (5 ml)	vanilla extract

Preheat the oven to 400°F (200°C). Grease a 12-cup muffin pan or line with paper muffin liners.

Measure the flour, sugar and baking powder into a medium bowl. In a small bowl, whisk together the egg, milk, oil or butter and vanilla, and add all at once to the flour mixture. Stir just until the flour is evenly moistened, but don't overmix—a few lumps are okay. Gently stir in any optional ingredients (see below) if desired.

Spoon batter into the prepared muffin pan, filling the cups to within ¼ inch (.5 cm) of the top. (You won't have enough batter to fill all 12 cups.) Bake in the preheated oven for 20 to 25 minutes, or until a toothpick poked into the middle of a muffin comes out clean.

Makes about 9 or 10 muffins.

Muffin options

Add one or two of the following ingredients to the basic muffin recipe. If using more than one ingredient, only add half the amount of each one.

1 cup (250 ml)	fresh or frozen blueberries (if frozen, don't thaw before using)
1 cup (250 ml)	fresh cranberries, halved
1 cup (250 ml)	chocolate chips
¾ cup (175 ml)	raisins or dried cranberries
¾ cup (175 ml)	chopped walnuts or pecans
¾ cup (50 ml)	poppy seeds

Beautiful Bran Muffins

Use regular unprocessed bran to make these muffins—not bran flakes or bran cereal. Bran is dirt cheap. A bag of it produces tons of muffins and will last you almost forever. And if you happen to plant a garden, you can sprinkle dry bran around your plants to keep the slugs away. You just never know.

¾ cup (175 ml)	light brown sugar
½ cup (125 ml)	vegetable oil
1	egg
1½ cups (375 ml)	unprocessed wheat bran (*not* bran flakes)
1 cup (250 ml)	all-purpose flour
1 tsp (5 ml)	baking soda
1 cup (250 ml)	buttermilk, yogurt or soured milk (see page 27)
½ cup (125 ml)	raisins or dried cranberries (optional)

Preheat the oven to 375°F (190°C). Grease a 12-cup muffin pan or line with paper muffin liners.

In a large bowl, whisk together the brown sugar, oil and egg until smooth. In another bowl, combine the bran, flour and the baking soda. Add the flour mixture to the egg mixture in 2 or 3 portions, alternating with the buttermilk, yogurt or soured milk, stirring just until everything is evenly moistened. Quickly stir in the raisins or cranberries if you're using them, just until they're mixed into the batter.

Spoon batter into the prepared muffin pan, filling the cups to within ¼ inch (.5 cm) of the top. (You won't have enough batter to fill all 12 cups.) Bake in the preheated oven for 20 to 25 minutes, or until a toothpick poked into the middle of a muffin comes out clean.

Makes about 10 muffins.

Banana Bread

You know those bananas you forgot to eat? The black ones? Give them another chance—make some banana bread.

1¼ cups (300 ml)	all-purpose flour
1 cup (250 ml)	granulated sugar
1 tsp (5 ml)	baking soda
½ cup (125 ml)	butter or vegetable oil
2	very ripe bananas
2	eggs

Preheat the oven to 350°F (180°C). Grease a 9 x 5-inch (23 x 13 cm) loaf pan.

In a large bowl, mix the flour, sugar and baking soda.

Put the butter or oil, the bananas and the eggs into the container of a blender or food processor and blend until smooth.

Pour the blended banana mixture into the flour mixture and stir until well mixed and smooth. Spoon into the prepared loaf pan and bake for 55 minutes to 1 hour—or until browned and a toothpick poked into the middle of the loaf comes out clean (with no batter clinging to it).

Makes 1 perfect loaf.

Muffin alternative

Use the same batter to make banana muffins, if you prefer. Grease cups of a muffin pan or line with paper liners, fill cups to within ¼ inch (.5 cm) of the top and bake for about 30 minutes, or until muffins test done with a toothpick.

> Chocolate chips? Raisins? Nuts? Go ahead and add ½ to 1 cup (125 to 250 ml) of any of them to the basic banana bread batter. You may never go back to plain banana bread again.

Corn Bread

Absolutely nothing goes better with a pot of chili than fresh corn bread.

1½ cups (375 ml)	all-purpose flour
1 cup (250 ml)	yellow cornmeal
¼ cup (50 ml)	granulated sugar
2 tbsp (30 ml)	baking powder
½ tsp (2 ml)	salt
¼ cup (50 ml)	vegetable oil
1	egg
1⅓ cups (325 ml)	milk

Preheat the oven to 350°F (180°C). Grease an 8- or 9-inch (20 or 23 cm) square baking dish.

In a large bowl, stir together the flour, cornmeal, sugar, baking powder and salt. In another bowl, whisk together the oil, egg and milk. Pour the milk mixture into the flour mixture and stir until just combined. A few lumps are okay, so don't beat the batter to death.

Pour batter into the prepared baking pan, spreading so that the top is even. Bake in the preheated oven for 15 to 20 minutes, or until lightly browned on top and a toothpick poked into the middle comes out clean.

Let cool for just a couple of minutes before cutting into squares.

Makes about 9 to 12 squares of corn bread.

Corn bread variations

Switch up your corn bread with a little something extra. Add any of the following ingredients when you combine the wet and dry mixtures:

½ cup (125 ml)	dried cranberries
1 cup (250 ml)	corn kernels (frozen, canned or cut from a cooked cob)
1 cup (250 ml)	shredded sharp cheddar cheese
1 or 2	chopped fresh jalapeño peppers or ¼ cup (50 ml) canned sliced jalapeños.
¼ cup (50 ml)	crumbled, crisply cooked bacon

Irish Soda Bread

This super-easy bread is traditionally made with buttermilk—a thick, tangy dairy product you'll find in the supermarket near the other kinds of milk. Use half the carton to make this bread, and the rest to make pancakes (page 25), bran muffins (page 159) or a delicious fruit smoothie for breakfast. If you can't get your hands on buttermilk, plain yogurt will do in a pinch. See yogurt option.

3¾ cups (850 ml)	all-purpose flour
¼ cup (50 ml)	light brown sugar
1½ tbsp (22 ml)	baking powder
½ tsp (2 ml)	baking soda
1 tsp (5 ml)	salt
¾ cup (175 ml)	raisins or dried cranberries (optional)
2 cups (500 ml)	buttermilk (or see yogurt option)
1	egg

Preheat the oven to 375°F (190°C). Grease a 9 x 5-inch (23 x 13 cm) loaf pan.

In a large bowl, combine the flour, brown sugar, baking powder, baking soda and salt. Add the raisins or cranberries, if you're using them.

In another bowl, stir together the buttermilk and egg. Working quickly, pour this mixture into the flour mixture, and stir until everything is blended. The dough will be pretty soft—that's okay. With your hands, mix the gucky dough in the bowl, adding a bit more flour if necessary so that you can handle it and shape it into a loaf. Place the loaf in the prepared pan and pat down so that the top is even. Bake in the preheated oven for 1 hour and 15 minutes, or until the loaf is nicely browned and a toothpick poked into the middle comes out clean, with no dough clinging to it. Remove from the pan and let cool for just a few minutes before devouring.

Butter? Are you kidding? Of course!

Makes 1 irresistibly delicious loaf.

Whole Wheat Soda Bread

Mix 2 cups (500 ml) whole wheat flour with 2 cups (500 ml) all-purpose flour for a brown version of this delicious bread.

Yogurt option

Stir together 1½ cups (175 ml) plain yogurt with ½ cup (125 ml) milk until smooth and pourable. Use instead of buttermilk.

Multipurpose Yeast Dough EF DF

Yeast. **Does that word scare you? Relax. This easy dough is the basis for all kinds of good things: pizza, focaccia, garlic bread sticks. Yeast is fun to work with, and everyone will think you're a genius. You just can't lose.**

3½ cups (800 ml)	all-purpose flour (approximately), divided
1 envelope	*quick-rise* instant yeast
1 tsp (5 ml)	salt
1 cup (250 ml)	hot tap water
2 tbsp (30 ml)	olive oil or vegetable oil

In a large bowl, stir together 2 cups (500 ml) of the flour, the yeast granules and the salt. Pour in the hot water and the oil, and stir until the mixture is smooth (it will be very gooey and sticky—don't worry). Gradually add the remaining flour, ½ cup (125 ml) at a time, stirring with a wooden spoon until stirring becomes difficult. You should still have some flour left.

Take the leftover flour and dump it onto the counter or table, then spread it around a bit. Turn the sticky lump of dough out onto this floured surface and begin kneading. This is the fun part. Squash the dough down with the heel of your hand, while turning and folding, over and over again, for 8 to 10 minutes. If the dough sticks to the counter, sprinkle with a little more flour. How do you know when the dough is ready? Pinch it gently between your fingers—when it feels like your earlobe, it's done. It should be smooth, stretchy and no longer sticky on the surface. (You may not need to use all the flour.)

Place the dough in an oiled bowl and turn it over to make sure all the sides are coated with oil. Cover with plastic wrap and place in a warm spot (see below) to rise until double in volume—about 30 minutes more or less.

When the dough has doubled in size, admire it for a minute, then make a fist and punch the dough right in the gizzard to deflate it. Turn it out of the bowl, knead it a few times and set it aside while you prepare to create something wonderful.

For more details, have a look at the recipes for focaccia (page 198), pizza (page 193) or garlic bread sticks (page 192).

See—that wasn't so hard, was it?

Yeast—the Bare Facts

Although yeast comes in various forms and types, we recommend that you use **quick-rise** instant yeast—a fast-acting form of active dry yeast. You mix the fine granules directly with the dry ingredients and the yeast begins to work much more quickly than ordinary dry yeast granules. You can find quick-rise instant yeast on the supermarket shelf near the other types. It comes in both small jars and individual premeasured envelopes. Unless you plan to do a lot of yeast baking, buying the envelopes makes more sense.

Getting a Rise out of Your Dough

The recipe tells you to let the dough rise in a warm spot. Where is that?

Check the top of your refrigerator. If it feels warmer than the surrounding air, that's a good spot.

Place a bowl or pot of very hot water on the bottom rack of your oven. Put the bowl of dough on the rack above it—but don't turn on the oven. Close the door—the hot water will keep the oven just warm enough to make the dough rise.

Place a large measuring cup of hot water in the microwave and nuke it until it begins to boil. Move the cup to a corner, put the bowl of dough into the microwave and close the door—but don't turn on the microwave. The warm, moist air in the microwave will do the trick.

Antidepressant Brownies

You flunked the geography test. You lost your favorite sweater. You had a fight with your best friend. It's raining. You need some brownies—fast.

1 cup (250 ml)	chocolate chips
⅔ cup (150 ml)	granulated sugar
⅓ cup (75 ml)	butter
2 tbsp (30 ml)	water
2	eggs
¾ cup (175 ml)	all-purpose flour
½ tsp (2 ml)	baking powder
1 tsp (5 ml)	vanilla extract
½ cup (125 ml)	coarsely chopped walnuts (optional—for severe depression)

Preheat the oven to 350°F (180°C). Grease an 8-inch (20 cm) square baking pan.

In a medium saucepan, combine the chocolate chips, sugar, butter and water. Place over low heat and cook, stirring constantly, just until the chocolate is melted and the mixture is smooth. Remove from heat and let cool for a couple of minutes.

Add the eggs to the chocolate mixture and whisk until smooth. Dump in the flour, baking powder and vanilla, and stir just until the dry ingredients have been incorporated, then add the chopped walnuts (if you're using them) and stir to mix. Pour into the prepared baking pan, and bake for 25 to 30 minutes—until a toothpick poked into the middle of the pan comes out nearly clean. Better to undercook slightly than overcook—so if you're not quite sure, then they're done.

Makes 20 to 25 doses—er, brownies.

Classic Chocolate Chip Cookies

Few things on this planet come even remotely close to the wonderfulness of a homemade chocolate chip cookie. Why don't you make a batch right now? You know you want to.

1 cup (250 ml)	butter, softened
¾ cup (175 ml)	granulated sugar
¾ cup (175 ml)	light brown sugar
2	eggs
1 tsp (5 ml)	vanilla
2¼ cups (550 ml)	all-purpose flour
1 tsp (5 ml)	baking soda
¼ tsp (1 ml)	salt
2 cups (500 ml)	semisweet chocolate chips
1 cup (250 ml)	chopped walnuts or pecans (optional)

Preheat the oven to 375°F (190°C).

In a large bowl, with an electric mixer (or in a food processor if you have one), beat together the butter with the granulated sugar, brown sugar, eggs and vanilla until nice and creamy.

In another bowl, combine the flour with the baking soda and salt. Add to the creamed mixture, beating until smooth and blended. Stir in the chocolate chips by hand. At this point, certain people might add nuts.

Drop the dough by teaspoonfuls onto an ungreased cookie sheet about 2 inches (5 cm) apart. Don't crowd the cookies—the baking time is short and you'll be baking several batches. Place in the preheated oven and bake for 10 to 12 minutes, or until the edges are just browned but the cookies are still a little soft in the middle. With a spatula, carefully remove the cookies to a cooling rack and repeat with the remaining dough. Try not to eat all the cookies before they're cool.

Makes 6 to 8 dozen, depending on the size and how much dough you ate.

Official Peanut Butter Cookies

Remember when you were little and your mom used to wait for you with a plate of peanut butter cookies and a glass of milk? No? Did anyone's mom ever do that? Well, you'll just have to make them for yourself.

½ cup (125 ml)	butter
½ cup (125 ml)	peanut butter
½ cup (125 ml)	granulated sugar
½ cup (125 ml)	light brown sugar
1	egg
1¼ cups (300 ml)	all-purpose or whole wheat flour
½ tsp (2 ml)	baking powder
½ tsp (2 ml)	baking soda
½ cup (125 ml)	chocolate chips (optional but recommended)

Preheat the oven to 375°F (190°C). Line a cookie sheet or two with aluminum foil or baking parchment paper.

In a large bowl, with an electric mixer, beat together the butter, peanut butter, granulated sugar, brown sugar and egg until smooth and creamy. Add the flour, baking powder and baking soda, and mix until smooth.

By hand, roll the dough into 1-inch (2 cm) balls and place them 2 inches (5 cm) apart on the prepared cookie sheet. Now, here's the crucial step: flatten each ball in a crisscross pattern with a fork. This detail is what makes them *official* peanut butter cookies. Do not, under any circumstances, forget to do this. Finally, if you haven't eaten all the chocolate chips, press 3 or 4 into each cookie if you want.

Bake in the preheated oven for 10 to 12 minutes, or until golden brown. The cookies will still be a bit soft, but they'll harden as they cool.

Makes about 3½ dozen.

No-Nonsense Coconut Oatmeal Cookies

Sort of plain, crisp, nothing weird about them at all. The perfect cookie for when you need something simple and good.

½ cup (125 ml)	butter, softened
½ cup (125 ml)	granulated sugar
½ cup (125 ml)	light brown sugar
1	egg
1 tsp (5 ml)	vanilla extract
1 cup (250 ml)	all-purpose or whole wheat flour
½ tsp (2 ml)	baking powder
½ tsp (2 ml)	baking soda
1 cup (250 ml)	unsweetened desiccated coconut
½ cup (125 ml)	quick-cooking rolled oats (not instant)

Preheat the oven to 375°F (190°C). Line a cookie sheet or two with aluminum foil or baking parchment paper.

In a large bowl, with an electric mixer, beat together the butter, granulated sugar, brown sugar, egg and vanilla until creamy. In another bowl, stir together the flour, baking powder and baking soda. Stir the flour mixture into the butter mixture (gradually, a scoop at a time) and mix until smooth. Finally, stir in the coconut and rolled oats.

Drop the batter by teaspoons onto the prepared cookie sheet, leaving 1½ inches (4 cm) between blobs to allow for spreading. Don't bother flattening them—they'll flatten themselves. Bake in the preheated oven for 10 to 12 minutes, or until lightly browned at the edges. With a spatula, remove to a rack. They'll become crisper as they cool.

Makes about 4 dozen cookies.

Desserts

Your guests will be polite enough through dinner. But we know they're all really waiting for dessert. Don't disappoint them.

Me? Make a pie? Are you kidding?

No. Not kidding. Here—try it.

First, prepare a batch of Foolproof Pastry Dough (see next page). To make the crust, sprinkle the counter or work area lightly with flour. Also dust 1 ball of the prepared dough with flour. Using a rolling pin, gently roll the dough out—first in one direction, then another, always working from the center of the ball outward. If the dough begins to stick to the rolling surface, sprinkle the surface with a little more flour. When the crust looks big enough, gently fold it in half and lift it carefully into your pie pan. Unfold it, and gently squish it down into the pan. Don't stretch it or tear it. Trim the excess dough from around the edges and do something fancy and frilly to them by pinching all the way around. Did you get a hole in your pastry? Patch it with a bit of leftover dough. No one will suspect.

Foolproof Pastry Dough EF DF

Even though you can buy prepared pastry, a homemade crust is a wonderful thing. Learning how to make one is worth it. You can use this easy pastry recipe to make everything from a fancy quiche for brunch to a perfect apple pie for dessert.

2 cups (500 ml)	flour
1 tsp (5 ml)	granulated sugar
⅔ cup (150 ml)	solid vegetable shortening (not butter or margarine)
1	egg
1 tsp (5 ml)	white or cider vinegar
	Ice water

Measure the flour and sugar into a bowl, and stir to mix. Cut the shortening up into chunks, and toss them into the bowl with the flour. Now, using a pastry blender (ask your mom) or two knives (one in each hand), chop the shortening into the flour until it looks all crumbly. The idea is to cut the shortening (the fat) up into teensy bits and mix it into the flour. Don't blend it the way you would cookie batter. The mixture should look something like uncooked oatmeal or bread crumbs.

Crack the egg into a measuring cup, add the vinegar and scramble until well mixed. Pour in enough ice water to equal a total of ½ cup (125 ml) of liquid. Add the liquid to the flour mixture and mix lightly, just until you can form the dough into a big ball. Don't overbeat—the dough should remain a bit lumpy. Divide the dough into 2 equal, smaller balls and flatten them a little, like hamburger patties. Wrap in plastic wrap and refrigerate for at least 1 hour.

When ready to use, remove from the refrigerator, roll out and have your way with them. You can use this pastry in any recipe that calls for a crust. If you don't need the second crust, wrap it tightly and freeze it to use at some other time.

Makes enough dough for 2 single-crust pie shells (bottom crusts only) or 1 double-crust pie (both bottom and top crusts).

There. A piece of cake—er, *pie*.

An Actual Pie Made by You

See—it's not that hard.

> 1 recipe   Foolproof Pastry Dough (page 170)
> 1 batch   prepared fruit (see box on next page) filling

Roll out 1 ball of pastry dough (half the recipe) on a well-floured surface, in a circle about 1½ inches (4 cm) larger all around than the pie pan you'll be using. (So—if you have a 9-inch pie pan, roll out the dough to a circle about 12 inches (30 cm) in diameter.) The edges may be a little rough—don't worry about it. Carefully fold the rolled dough in half and lift it gently into the pie pan. Unfold and fit it evenly into the pan without stretching it. Some dough will overhang the edges. Using a sharp knife, cut the dough even with the rim of the pan.

In a large bowl, prepare your fruit filling. Dump it into the crust, mounding the fruit higher in the middle than around the sides.

Roll the rest of the pastry dough out (the other half of the recipe), again on a well-floured surface, into another circle about the same size as the first. Fold the pastry in half, lift it carefully and gently place it onto the filled crust. Unfold so that it covers the filling and let the edges drape over the sides. Leaving a small amount of overhang, trim the excess so that the crust is even all around. Now, very gently, tuck the edges of the top crust under the edges of the bottom crust in order to keep everything enclosed. With your fingers, firmly pinch the edges together to make a frilly-looking border. Cut 3 or 4 slits in the top of the crust as steam vents.

Preheat the oven to 375°F (190°C). Put pie on a larger cookie sheet or pizza pan (to catch any messy boil-overs in the oven).

Place in the preheated oven and bake for 50 to 60 minutes, or until the fruit is tender and bubbling. Poke a knife in through one of the steam vents to check on the doneness of the fruit.

Wow—did *you* make that?

Fruit Pie Fillings ...

Apple

5 cups (1.25 l)	peeled, cored and thinly sliced apples
¾ cup (175 ml)	granulated sugar
2 tbsp (30 ml)	all-purpose flour
½ tsp (2 ml)	cinnamon

Peach

5 cups (1.25 l)	peeled, pitted and sliced peaches
¾ cup (175 ml)	granulated sugar
2 tbsp (30 ml)	all-purpose flour
2 tbsp (30 ml)	cornstarch
½ tsp (2 ml)	cinnamon (optional)

Rhubarb (or Rhubarb and Strawberry)

5 cups (1.25 l)	diced fresh rhubarb stalks (or go half rhubarb and half sliced strawberries)
1 cup (250 ml)	granulated sugar
2 tbsp (30 ml)	all-purpose flour
2 tbsp (30 ml)	cornstarch

Blueberry

5 cups (1.25l)	fresh or frozen blueberries, stemmed
¾ cup (175 ml)	granulated sugar
2 tbsp (30 ml)	all-purpose flour
2 tbsp (30 ml)	cornstarch
1 tsp (5 ml)	grated lemon zest (optional)

Bread Pudding

You know that old bread you were about to put out for the birds? Well, hang on just a second. Make this instead. The birds can wait.

4 cups (1 l)	bread cubes, any kind (slightly stale is fine, but *moldy* is not)
½ cup (125 ml)	raisins
3 cups (750 ml)	milk
4	eggs
½ cup (125 ml)	granulated sugar
1 tsp (5 ml)	vanilla
½ tsp (2 ml)	cinnamon

Grease a 9 x 13-inch (23 x 33 cm) rectangular baking dish.

Place the bread cubes and raisins in the baking dish and toss to mix.

In a bowl, beat together the milk, eggs, sugar, vanilla and cinnamon. Pour this mixture over the bread cubes, cover with plastic wrap, refrigerate and let soak for several hours or overnight.

When ready to bake, preheat the oven to 325°F (160°C). Unwrap pudding, place in the preheated oven and bake for 40 to 45 minutes, or until puffed and golden. Sprinkle with icing sugar (for fanciness) and serve warm with ice cream or whipped cream if you have any.

Makes 6 to 8 servings.

Baked Apples GF EF

A nice, squishy baked apple is a very virtuous dessert. If you don't want to feel so virtuous, have some ice cream with it.

6	medium apples (Macintosh, Spy, Cortland and Idared are good apples for baking)
½ cup (125 ml)	sugar
¼ tsp (1 ml)	cinnamon
2 tbsp (30 ml)	butter
1 cup (250 ml)	boiling water

Preheat the oven to 400°F (200°C). Grease a baking dish just big enough to hold all the apples comfortably.

Wash and core the apples from the stem end down, almost but *not quite* all the way through to the bottom. Pull out the core and discard it. Remove a strip of peel from the equator of each apple, about a third of the way down from the top (this prevents the apple from splitting when it bakes). Arrange the apples, cavity-side up, in the prepared baking dish.

In a small bowl, combine the sugar and the cinnamon. Fill the cavity of each apple almost to the top with this mixture, then seal the top with a dab of butter.

Pour the boiling water into the dish around the apples, place in the preheated oven and bake for 40 to 45 minutes, or until very tender, basting every so often with the liquid in the pan.

Let the apples cool slightly before serving, then serve warm or at room temperature with ice cream, or just plain with a spoonful of the baking liquid drizzled over top.

Makes 6 servings.

Self-Saucing Hot Fudge Pudding EF

Save this deadly dessert for moments of deepest chocolate desperation. Beware—this is not for the timid.

1 cup (250 ml)	all-purpose flour
1½ cups (375 ml)	granulated sugar, divided
2 tsp (10 ml)	baking powder
½ cup (125 ml)	vegetable oil
½ cup (125 ml)	unsweetened cocoa powder, divided
½ cup (125 ml)	milk
1 tsp (5 ml)	vanilla
½ cup (125 ml)	chopped walnuts or pecans
1¾ cups (425 ml)	hot water

Preheat the oven to 350°F (180°C). Grease a 9-inch (23 cm) square baking dish.

In the prepared baking dish, stir together the flour, ¾ cup (175 ml) of the sugar (*half* the total amount of sugar) and the baking powder. In a small bowl, stir together the vegetable oil and ¼ cup (50 ml) of the cocoa (*half* the total amount of cocoa). Add the cocoa mixture to the flour mixture along with the milk and the vanilla. Stir with a fork until combined.

In another bowl, stir together the remaining ¾ cup (175 ml) of the sugar, the remaining ¼ cup (50 ml) of the cocoa and the chopped nuts. Sprinkle this mixture evenly over the stuff in the pan—*don't mix it in.* Now carefully pour the hot water over everything—don't mess with it, don't stir it. Place in the preheated oven and bake for 40 to 45 minutes, or until the top is crusty and a bubbly chocolate sauce has formed in the dish. Serve warm with vanilla ice cream.

Makes 6 servings, but I wouldn't count on it.

Crème Caramel GF

You want to make a sophisticated dessert—elegant, yet understated. Something French-ish and impressive. Something that appears tricky to produce, but isn't. Here you go.

¾ cup (175 ml)	granulated sugar, divided
3	eggs
2½ cups (625 ml)	milk, heated until hot but not boiling
½ tsp (2 ml)	vanilla

Preheat the oven to 350°F (180°C). Have ready six ½-cup (125 ml) glass or pottery custard cups. Arrange these in a baking pan large enough to hold all of them comfortably.

In your smallest, heaviest saucepan, heat ½ cup (125 ml) of the sugar over medium heat, stirring constantly. First the sugar will do nothing, then the whole business will go all clumpy and weird, then—amazingly—the sugar will melt and turn into a golden syrup. Don't try to hurry this process, because sugar burns easily. Remove the pan from the heat as soon as the syrup turns golden and pour it into the prepared custard cups, dividing the syrup evenly among the cups and swirling the cups so the syrup coats the bottoms and sides. The syrup will solidify as it cools.

Beat the eggs with the remaining ¼ cup (50 ml) of the sugar. Add the hot milk and vanilla, and stir until the sugar is dissolved. Pour into the prepared custard cups (the melted sugar will have solidified to coat the cups), dividing the mixture evenly.

Boil some water in a saucepan or kettle. Pour boiling water into the large baking pan in which the custard cups are sitting—the water should come about halfway up the sides of the cups. The idea is to create a water bath around the custard cups so that they bake slowly and evenly. Put the entire pan (water and custard cups) into the preheated oven, and bake for 50 minutes to 1 hour, or until a knife poked into the middle of one of the cups comes out clean, with nothing stuck to it.

Cool your crème caramels to room temperature, then refrigerate for several hours or, preferably, overnight. When you're ready to serve, run a thin knife around the edge of each custard to loosen it from its cup. Place a plate over top and unmold each one gently. During the baking and chilling process the melted sugar coating will have liquefied into a sauce which you can now pour or spoon over the custards as you serve them. Repeat with the remaining custards. Prepare to take a bow.

Makes 6 servings.

Rainy Day Rice Pudding GF EF

Though recommended for rainy days, this rice pudding is also suitable for blinding snowstorms, sleet, even minor hurricanes—as long as the power doesn't go out.

3 cups (750 ml)	milk, heated to almost boiling
⅓ cup (75 ml)	short grain rice (arborio or Italian-style rice is recommended)
¼ cup (50 ml)	granulated sugar
2 tbsp (30 ml)	butter
¼ cup (50 ml)	raisins (optional)
1 tsp (5 ml)	vanilla
	Cinnamon for sprinkling

Preheat the oven to 250°F (120°C). Grease an 8-cup (2 l) ovenproof casserole dish (any shape).

In a bowl, stir together the milk, rice, sugar and butter. Pour into the prepared casserole dish and place in the preheated oven. Bake for about 2½ hours, stirring every half hour or so. Add the raisins (if you're using them) and vanilla in the last 30 minutes of baking. Remove from the oven, let cool slightly and serve warm. Or chill and serve cold. Sprinkle each serving with a bit of cinnamon, and eat while sitting in a squishy chair, watching the rain drip down the window.

Makes 4 servings.

Bananas Flambé EF

Now, this is fun. Really fun. That it also happens to be a crazy delicious dessert is almost beside the point.

4	large, ripe bananas, peeled, cut in half crosswise, then split in half lengthwise
2 tsp (10 ml)	lemon juice
3 tbsp (45 ml)	butter
½ cup (125 ml)	light brown sugar
3 tbsp (45 ml)	brandy or liqueur, any kind
	Vanilla ice cream

Sprinkle the bananas with the lemon juice to prevent them from turning brown and place them in a bowl.

Melt the butter in a large skillet over medium heat and stir in the brown sugar. Add the bananas to the pan and cook for about 3 minutes or until almost tender, turning them over carefully once. Remove the pan from heat.

Put on your oven mitts and turn off the lights.

Okay. Here's the good part. Pour the brandy or liqueur over the bananas (still in the skillet) and immediately light a match or lighter (a long fireplace match or barbecue lighter keeps your hand away from the flame) and set the bananas on fire. Actually, it's just the brandy that ignites, but it's pretty exciting anyway. Enjoy the show, allow the flame to die out by itself and then spoon the bananas and syrupy sauce over a dish of vanilla ice cream.

Makes 4 thrilling servings.

Apple (or Other) Crisp EF

Everyone knows about apple crisp. But what about peach or rhubarb or blueberry or pear or plum? Live on the edge—try a combination.

6	medium apples, peeled, cored and cut into chunks (or 4 cups/1 l of any prepared fruit)
½ cup (125 ml)	granulated sugar
1 tsp (5 ml)	cinnamon, divided
½ cup (125 ml)	brown sugar
½ cup (125 ml)	butter, softened
½ cup (125 ml)	quick-cooking rolled oats (not instant)

Preheat the oven to 375°F (190°C). Grease a 9-inch (23 cm) square or round baking dish.

Dump the apple slices into the prepared baking dish, add the granulated sugar and about half the cinnamon. Toss until well mixed.

In a mixing bowl, combine the brown sugar, butter, oats and the rest of the cinnamon, mashing everything together with a fork until it forms a crumbly mixture. Sprinkle this over the apples in the pan. Place in the preheated oven and bake for 40 to 45 minutes, or until the apples are very soft when you poke them with a fork. You must serve this warm with vanilla ice cream. It's the law.

Leftovers (you can only hope) make an amazing breakfast.

Serves 6 to 8. Or less.

Useless but Fun

Remember the famous Volcano Project from fourth grade? You add some vinegar to some baking soda, and bingo! Instant Vesuvius! Try it—it'll make you feel like a kid again.

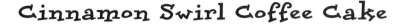

Cinnamon Swirl Coffee Cake

Is there anything that smells as warm and homey as something with cinnamon baking in the oven? And the cake tastes pretty great too. It's a win–win.

½ cup (125 ml)	light brown sugar
2 tbsp (30 ml)	vegetable oil
1 tsp (5 ml)	vanilla
1	egg
1¼ cups (300 ml)	flour
2 tsp (10 ml)	baking powder
¾ cup (175 ml)	milk
½ cup (125 ml)	granulated sugar
1 tsp (5 ml)	cinnamon

Preheat the oven to 350°F (180°C). Grease an 8-inch (20 cm) square baking pan.

In a medium bowl, beat together the brown sugar, oil, vanilla and egg just until well mixed.

In another bowl, stir together the flour and baking powder.

Add the flour mixture to the egg mixture in two or three additions, alternating each addition with the milk and mixing well after each one. Dump the batter into the prepared baking pan, spreading the top smooth.

Mix the granulated sugar with the cinnamon. Sprinkle the cinnamon sugar over the cake batter in the pan. Using a knife, gently swirl the cinnamon sugar through the batter, folding it over in places, but leaving it unevenly mixed. You should have some spots where the sugar is on the surface and other spots where it's marbled into the batter.

Place in the preheated oven and bake for 25 to 30 minutes, or until the edges are lightly browned and a toothpick poked into the middle comes out clean, with no batter clinging to it.

Serve warm or at room temperature.

Makes 6 to 8 servings.

Speedy Apple Cake

A fast, goofproof dessert—easier than a pie and tasty enough to make everyone happy.

5	apples, peeled, cored, and thinly sliced
¾ cup (175 ml)	granulated sugar, divided
1 tsp (5 ml)	cinnamon
2 tbsp (30 ml)	butter
1	egg
½ cup (125 ml)	flour
1 tsp (5 ml)	baking powder

Preheat the oven to 350°F (180°C). Grease a 9-inch (23 cm) round or square baking dish.

Dump the apples into the prepared baking dish and sprinkle with ¼ cup (50 ml) of the sugar and all the cinnamon.

In a mixing bowl, beat together the butter and the remaining ½ cup (125 ml) sugar. Add the egg, mix well, then add the flour and baking powder. Beat until smooth. Drop this batter by spoonfuls over the apples. There won't be enough batter to cover the apples completely— that's okay. Just leave part of the apples exposed (*eek!*). Place in the preheated oven and bake for 45 minutes, or until the apples are soft and the cake is browned.

There. Dessert just doesn't get much easier.

Makes 4 to 6 servings.

Baking Powder, Baking Soda— What's the Difference, Anyway?

If the recipe calls for baking powder, *no*, you can't use baking soda instead. Or vice versa. Here's why: when you mix baking soda (also known as sodium bicarbonate) with an acid ingredient (such as vinegar, lemon juice or yogurt) a chemical reaction takes place, creating little carbon dioxide bubbles that make your pancakes (for instance) nice and fluffy. Baking powder, on the other hand, is already a mixture of baking soda and an acid, so it bubbles with no help whatsoever. In addition, baking powder also reacts to heat, causing it to double-bubble—first when you mix it into the batter and again when you cook it. The two products work differently and can't be substituted for each other. So pay attention!

Desperate for Cheesecake

If this cheesecake is too much work for you, then you're obviously not desperate enough. Yet.

Crust

1½ cups (375 ml)	graham cracker crumbs
⅓ cup (75 ml)	melted butter
¼ cup (50 ml)	granulated sugar

Filling

2 pkgs (8 oz/250 g each)	cream cheese, softened
½ cup (125 ml)	sugar
1 tsp (5 ml)	vanilla
2	eggs

Preheat the oven to 350°F (180°C).

In a bowl, stir together the crust ingredients: the graham cracker crumbs, melted butter and sugar. Press into the bottom and up the sides of a 9-inch (23 cm) pie plate. If you happen to own two pie plates, you can squish one into the other with the crumb mixture in between to get the crust smooth and even.

Now make the filling. In a large bowl, with an electric mixer, beat together the cream cheese, sugar and vanilla until well blended. Add the eggs, one at a time, and keep beating for another couple of minutes, until the filling is smooth. Pour into the graham cracker crust. Bake in the preheated oven for 40 to 45 minutes, until set. The center of the cheesecake should still be a bit soft, so don't overbake. Refrigerate for at least 3 hours (or as long as overnight) before serving.

Top with fresh fruit (like strawberries, blueberries or peaches) or your favorite ready-made pie filling. Purists, of course, may prefer to have the cheesecake plain.

Makes 1 serving. Just kidding.

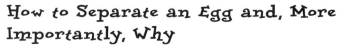

How to Separate an Egg and, More Importantly, Why

Some recipes ask you to do this. Why? Because some recipes call for only the yolk or the white, or tell you to beat the two parts of the egg separately. You won't be doing this sort of thing often, but it's good to know how to do it if ever you need to.

Find a medium-size funnel. (There's probably one in that scary junk drawer you hate.) Stand the funnel upright in a measuring cup, and *very carefully* crack the egg into it. Don't break the yolk! Lift the funnel up and gently jiggle it until the white slides out the hole, leaving the yolk stranded in the top. Dump the yolk out into one bowl and the white into another. Repeat if you need more than one egg separated.

How to Make Whipped Cream

Sure, whipped cream in a spray can is oodles of fun, but honest to goodness home-whipped cream is something else altogether. Not only does the real thing taste better, but it doesn't deflate and go all watery on your cake like the spray stuff.

Start with a container of very cold whipping cream or heavy cream. Pour it into a bowl and add a spoonful or two of sugar. Using an electric mixer, beat the cream until it stands up in soft peaks when you lift the beater out. Stop beating as soon as the cream is whipped. If you continue, it will eventually turn into butter (did you know that?). That's nice—but not what you had in mind, is it?

Helpful whipping hints: the colder everything is when you whip cream, the better it works. The cream should be straight from the refrigerator. And if you really want to go all out, refrigerate the bowl and the beaters for a few minutes before whipping.

Go ahead—lick the beaters.

Pineapple Upside-Down Cake

Who thought this up, anyway? Do you suppose it was an accident?

1 can (14 oz/398 ml)	sliced pineapple rings, packed in juice
⅓ cup (75 ml)	butter, divided
½ cup (125 ml)	brown sugar
½ cup (125 ml)	granulated sugar
1	egg
1 tsp (5 ml)	vanilla
1 cup (250 ml)	flour
1½ tsp (7 ml)	baking powder

Preheat the oven to 350°F (180°C).

Drain the pineapple, but save the juice from the can in a small bowl.

Melt 2 tbsp (30 ml) of the butter and pour it into an 8-inch (20 cm) baking pan. Stir in the brown sugar and 1 tbsp (15 ml) of the pineapple juice, and spread the mixture to cover the bottom of the baking pan. Arrange the pineapple rings as artistically as possible in the pan, cutting them in half if necessary (to create a suitably tasteful design).

In a bowl, with an electric mixer, beat together the remaining butter and granulated sugar until creamy. Add the egg and vanilla, and beat well.

In another bowl, mix the flour and baking powder. Add the flour mixture in two or three additions, alternating with ½ cup (125 ml) of the reserved pineapple juice and beating well after each addition. Spread the batter over the pineapple creation in the pan and bake in the preheated oven for 40 to 45 minutes, or until lightly browned.

While you're waiting, you can drink any leftover pineapple juice.

At the end of the baking time, remove cake from the oven. Cool the upside-down cake (which is still right-side up at this point) for 5 minutes, then run a knife around the edges of the pan to loosen it. Hold a plate over the pan and, all at once, flip the thing over. The upside-down cake should now be properly upside-down, and your artwork should be clearly visible—if somewhat transformed. If any stubborn pineapple pieces cling to the pan, just scrape them off and stick them back on the cake. No one will know. Serve warm.

Makes 6 to 8 servings.

Carrot Cake with Cream Cheese Icing

Who else but a mom could possibly have thought to put carrots in a cake and cream cheese in the frosting? This is a classic.

2 cups (500 ml)	all-purpose flour
2 tsp (10 ml)	baking powder
1½ tsp (7 ml)	baking soda
1 tsp (5 ml)	cinnamon
2 cups (500 ml)	granulated sugar
1 cup (250 ml)	vegetable oil
4	eggs
2 cups (500 ml)	coarsely grated carrots
1 cup (250 ml)	canned crushed pineapple, well drained
½ cup (125 ml)	chopped walnuts or pecans

Preheat the oven to 350°F (180°C). Grease a 9 x 13-inch (23 x 33 cm) rectangular baking pan, or line it with baking parchment paper. (See page 186 for more details.)

In a medium bowl, stir together the flour, baking powder, baking soda and cinnamon. In a large bowl, beat together the sugar, oil and eggs until creamy. Add the flour mixture to the egg mixture, stir, then add the carrots, pineapple and nuts. Spread the batter in the prepared baking pan. Place in the preheated oven and bake for 40 to 45 minutes, or until a toothpick poked into the middle comes out clean, with no batter clinging to it.

Remove the cake from the oven, let it cool for just a minute or two, then run a thin knife around the sides of the pan to loosen the cake. Invert it onto a cooling rack. (If you don't have a rack, you can invert the cake onto a tray or pan instead.) Peel off the paper (if you're using it) and let cool completely (I mean it!) before frosting with cream cheese icing.

Makes 10 to 12 servings.

Cream Cheese Icing

2 cups (500 ml)	icing sugar
½ cup (125 ml)	cream cheese, softened
¼ cup (50 ml)	butter, softened

In a medium bowl, with an electric mixer, beat together icing sugar, cream cheese and butter until fluffy and smooth.

Makes enough icing to frost a 9 x 13 (23 x 33 cm) cake.

Almond Torte with Mocha Cream Icing

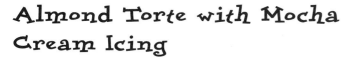

And now for something completely different—yet completely delicious. It shouldn't work, but somehow it does.

4	eggs
¾ cup (175 ml)	sugar
1 cup (250 ml)	whole almonds
2 tbsp (30 ml)	flour
2½ tsp (12 ml)	baking powder

Preheat the oven to 350°F (180°C). Grease two 8-inch (20 cm) round cake pans and line them with baking parchment paper. (See page 186 for details.)

In the container of a blender, combine the eggs and sugar. Whirl at high speed until the mixture is smooth. Now add the almonds—yes, whole. Put the lid back on the container and blend until the nuts are very finely ground. Pulverized, actually. Add the flour and the baking powder, and blend just until combined. Pour the batter into the prepared cake pans, place in the oven and bake for about 15 to 18 minutes, or cakes are springy and lightly browned.

Remove from the oven and let the cakes cool for about 5 minutes. Run a knife around the edge of the pan to loosen the cake, then invert it onto a metal cooling rack. (If you don't have a rack, a plate will do.) Peel off the paper and let the cake cool completely before frosting top, sides and between the layers in an elegant and tasteful manner.

Mocha Whipped Cream Icing

1½ cups (375 ml)	heavy or whipping cream
½ cup (125 ml)	granulated sugar
¼ cup (50 ml)	unsweetened cocoa powder
2 tsp (10 ml)	vanilla
1 tbsp (15 ml)	instant coffee

Combine the cream, sugar, cocoa powder, vanilla and instant coffee in a mixing bowl, and beat with an electric mixer until the mixture is thick and forms peaks when you lift the beater.

This makes enough to spread generously on the top, sides and between the two layers of an 8-inch (20 cm) round cake.

Be nice—share the beaters with a friend.

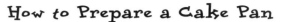

How to Prepare a Cake Pan

Nothing is more annoying than a cake that refuses to exit the baking pan. Okay, some things are more annoying—but not many. The following (unbelievably easy) method is guaranteed to help you avoid the dreaded Stuck Cake Syndrome.

Cut a sheet of baking parchment paper or waxed paper to fit your baking pan—use a pencil to trace around the pan so that the paper will fit on the bottom inside. Now lightly grease the pan (sides and bottom) with some solid vegetable shortening, butter or commercial nonstick cooking spray. Place the waxed paper liner in the pan and lightly grease both the paper and the sides thoroughly.

That's all you have to do. Pour in the batter and bake the cake as usual.

To remove your cake from the pan, run a knife around the sides of the cake to loosen it, invert the pan onto a metal rack or a platter—and the cake will drop right out. It really will drop right out. Peel off the paper, and away you go.

How to Measure Butter

Measuring butter is one of those stupid jobs that no one likes to do. The butter sticks to the cup, it doesn't pack down easily, it's just annoying. Here's a trick to make the job easier. Let's say your recipe asks for half a cup of butter. Fill a measuring cup to the ½ cup level with cold *(important detail!)* water. Scoop in the butter, any which way, until it fills the cup all the way to the 1 cup mark. Drain off the water (completely) and—voilà! You have a ½ cup of butter. (Different quantities of butter will require you to do a little math.) You can use this trick to measure other solid fats, such as vegetable shortening, margarine or lard, since these substances don't dissolve in water. But don't try it with sugar, kids.

Idiotproof One-Bowl Chocolate Cake

It's probably possible to mess up this easy cake—but you'd really have to work at it. And why on earth would anyone do such a thing? This cake is dark, rich, perfect.

2 cups (500 ml)	granulated sugar
1¾ cups (425 ml)	all-purpose flour
¾ cup (175 ml)	unsweetened cocoa powder
1½ tsp (7 ml)	baking powder
1½ tsp (7 ml)	baking soda
2	eggs
1 cup (250 ml)	milk
½ cup (125 ml)	vegetable oil
2 tsp (10 ml)	vanilla
1 cup (250 ml)	boiling water

Preheat the oven to 350°F (180°C). Grease two 8- or 9-inch (20 or 23 cm) round cake pans and line them with baking parchment paper or waxed paper (see page 186 for foolproof details).

In a large bowl, combine the sugar, flour, cocoa, baking powder and baking soda. Add the eggs, milk, oil and vanilla, and beat with an electric mixer for about 2 minutes. (If you don't have an electric mixer, you can whisk the batter by hand until smooth.) Add the boiling water and beat or whisk just until combined. This batter is quite liquidy—that's normal.

Pour the batter into the prepared pans, dividing it equally. Place in the preheated oven and bake for 30 to 35 minutes, or until a toothpick stuck into the middle of each cake comes out clean. Run a knife around the edge of each cake to loosen it from the pan, invert the pan onto a metal rack (or a plate if you don't have a rack)—and the cake should just drop out. Peel off the waxed paper and let the cake cool completely before icing. *Completely.*

Makes two 8- or 9-inch (20 or 23 cm) round cake layers.

 # Idiotproof One-Bowl Yellow Cake

The vanilla yin to the chocolate yang. Or is it the other way around? Whatever. This is just as idiotproof and just as good.

3	eggs
1½ cups (375 ml)	granulated sugar
1½ tsp (7 ml)	vanilla
1½ cups (375 ml)	all-purpose flour
1½ tsp (7 ml)	baking powder
¾ cup (175 ml)	milk, heated to boiling
¼ cup (50 ml)	vegetable oil

Preheat the oven to 350°F (180°C). Grease two 8- or 9-inch (20 or 23 cm) round cake pans and line them with baking parchment paper or waxed paper (see page 186 for foolproof details).

In a large bowl, with an electric mixer, beat the eggs for 1 or 2 minutes, until foamy. Add the sugar and vanilla, and continue beating until light and fluffy, about 5 minutes. Add the flour and baking powder, and beat just until combined. Finally, add the hot milk and vegetable oil, and beat until smooth. Pour the batter evenly into the prepared pans, and bake in the preheated oven for 20 to 25 minutes, or until the tops are golden and a toothpick poked into the middle of the cakes comes out clean, with no batter clinging to it.

Loosen the sides of the cakes by running a knife around the edge of each pan, then invert the pans on a rack—the cakes should fall out. Peel off the waxed paper and let cakes cool completely before icing.

Done.

Makes two 8- or 9-inch (20 or 23 cm) round cake layers.

Frostings (Not from a Can)

So there you are. You've made a cake from scratch. You are feeling very proud of yourself—and rightly so. Now, are you really going to use a canned frosting? We think not.

Chocolate Frosting GF EF

1 cup (250 ml)	butter, softened
2 cups (500 ml)	icing sugar (also known as confectioner's sugar)
½ cup (125 ml)	unsweetened cocoa powder
¼ tsp (1 ml)	vanilla
1 tbsp (15 ml)	milk (more, if needed)

In a large bowl with an electric mixer, beat the butter until creamy. Add the icing sugar, cocoa powder, vanilla and milk, and beat well, until smooth and fluffy. If the icing seems too thick, add a little more milk, just a few drops at a time, until the icing has a nice, spreadable consistency. Remember—you can always add *more* milk, but you can't take it out if you've added too much.

See? That wasn't very difficult, was it?

This makes exactly the right amount of frosting to ice the tops, sides and middle of a two-layer, 8- or 9-inch (20 or 23 cm) round cake, with just enough left over to lick off the beaters.

Vanilla Frosting GF EF

1 cup (250 ml)	butter, softened
3 cups (750 ml)	icing sugar (also known as confectioner's sugar)
1 tsp (5 ml)	vanilla
2 tbsp (30 ml)	milk

In a food processor, or in a large bowl using an electric mixer, beat the butter until creamy. Add the icing sugar, vanilla and milk, and beat well—until very fluffy and smooth. If the icing seems too thick, add a little more milk, just a few drops at a time, until it has a nice, spreadable consistency.

There.

This makes exactly the right amount of frosting to ice the tops, sides and middle of a two-layer, 8- or 9-inch (20 or 23 cm) round cake. Share the beaters with a friend.

Snacks and Munchies

 ## High-Voltage Garlic Bread EF

Don't munch this before a big date. Unless, of course, you've both been eating it.

1	long French baguette or Italian ciabatta loaf
4 to 6 cloves	garlic, minced or pressed
2 tbsp (30 ml)	olive oil
2 tbsp (30 ml)	chopped fresh parsley
2 tbsp (30 ml)	grated Parmesan cheese
½ tsp (2 ml)	paprika

Preheat oven to 400°F (200°C).

In a small bowl, combine the garlic and oil, mashing them together well. In another bowl, mix the chopped parsley, Parmesan cheese and paprika.

With a sharp bread knife, cut the bread in half crosswise, then cut each half horizontally in half as evenly as you can (don't obsess—it's only bread). This will give you 4 longish slabs of bread. Brush the garlic–oil mixture onto the cut surfaces of the bread, using it all up. Sprinkle, likewise, with the parsley mixture.

Put the bread on a baking sheet, garlic-side up, and bake for 10 minutes, until lightly browned on top and heated all the way through. Please, oh please, oh please, don't leave the room while this is in the oven. In fact, don't answer the phone, don't read a book, don't do anything. A minute too long in the oven and the bread is, um, toast. Or worse.

Cut into chunks and serve.

Makes 4 to 6 servings.

Tomato and Basil Bruschetta EF DF

Make this in the summer when tomatoes really taste like tomatoes (not just red tennis balls) and fresh basil is easy to find.

3	perfectly ripe medium tomatoes
2 cloves	garlic, squished
2 tbsp (30 ml)	chopped fresh basil
1 tsp (5 ml)	salt
¼ tsp (1 ml)	black pepper
1	long French loaf or Italian bread
¼ cup (50 ml)	olive oil

Preheat the broiler element of your oven. Place the top oven rack in the highest possible position.

Chop the tomatoes as finely as you can and put them in a mixing bowl. Add the garlic, basil, salt and pepper. Mix well.

With a sharp bread knife, cut the bread crosswise in half, then cut each half in half lengthwise. This will give you 4 long slabs of bread. Lay them, cut-side up, on a large baking sheet. Using a pastry brush (or clean paintbrush), brush the cut side of each slab of bread with some of the olive oil. Place on the top oven rack under the preheated broiler and toast the top of the bread for 3 to 5 minutes, just until golden brown. Don't leave the room. Don't answer the phone. Don't do anything. One minute too long under the broiler and the bread is charcoal. Remove from oven immediately.

Spoon the tomato mixture over the toasted bread, cut into 3-inch (7 cm) chunks and serve to your adoring fans.

This really makes 4 or 5 servings as an appetizer, but you might just find yourself eating the whole works by yourself for dinner.

Bruschetta variations

Sprinkle some grated Parmesan cheese over the tomato mixture.

Top the toasted bread with thinly sliced fresh mozzarella cheese (bocconcini) before adding the tomatoes.

Add a chopped fresh hot pepper to the tomato mixture.

Lay a thin slice of prosciutto on the toasted bread before topping with the tomato mixture.

Dastardly Garlic Bread Sticks

Dreadfully good, perilously addictive and frighteningly easy to make.

1 recipe	Multipurpose Yeast Dough (see page 163)
4 cloves	garlic, minced or pressed
¼ cup (50 ml)	olive oil
1 tbsp (15 ml)	coarse or kosher salt

Grease two cookie sheets.

Divide the dough into 4 blobs, and roll each one into a long snake no more than ½ inch (1 cm) thick. Cut the snake into 4 pieces, and arrange them on the prepared cookie sheets, making sure they don't touch one another. If all has gone according to plan, you should have 16 ropes of dough—8 on each cookie sheet.

In a small bowl, mash the garlic with the oil. Using a pastry brush or clean paintbrush, brush the bread sticks with the garlic oil on one side, then turn them over and brush the other side. Sprinkle the tops lightly with the salt.

Cover the pans loosely with plastic wrap and let rise in a warm spot for 20 to 30 minutes—or until puffy. They don't have to double in volume.

Preheat your oven to 375°F (190°C).

Remove the plastic wrap from the baking sheets, place the sheets in the oven and bake the bread sticks for 10 to 15 minutes, or until the bottoms are lightly browned and the top crust is golden.

These are best served straight from the oven, with soup or salad or dip. But they're good cold too if any happen to be left over (don't count on it).

Makes about 16 dastardly bread sticks.

Pizza from the Ground Up

Make your own pizza and your friends will think you are brilliant. Make your own pizza with a *homemade* crust and they will think you are a god.

The Crust

Begin with a batch of Multipurpose Yeast Dough (recipe on page 163). One recipe will make two 12-inch (30 cm) pizzas or a single mammoth pizza. You can use half the dough right away and freeze the other half (tightly wrapped in plastic) to use later, or you can make two pizzas right away—bake one immediately and freeze the other (unbaked) for a future pizza emergency. So many excellent choices.

If you don't have time to make the dough for a homemade pizza crust, you still have plenty of options. See next page for alternative pizza crust possibilities.

Creating the Pizza

The following ingredients are just suggestions—so don't take them too seriously. Add or subtract anything and everything—the procedure is the same no matter what you put on your pizza. The amounts are also approximate. For each pizza, choose no more than 4 or 5 toppings.

1 cup (250 ml)	spaghetti sauce (homemade or store-bought)
2 cups (500 ml)	shredded cheese (mozzarella, cheddar, provolone, Asiago, fontina—whatever kind you like, even a mixture)
1 cup (250 ml)	sliced fresh mushrooms
1 cup (250 ml)	sliced pepperoni
1 cup (250 ml)	crumbled cooked bacon
1 cup (250 ml)	crumbled cooked sausage
½ cup (125 ml)	chopped green pepper
½ cup (125 ml)	chopped onion
½ cup (125 ml)	sliced olives
½ cup (125 ml)	pineapple chunks
¼ cup (50 ml)	torn fresh basil leaves
1 tsp (5 ml)	oregano
½ tsp (2 ml)	hot pepper flakes

Preheat the oven to 450°F (230°C). Grease two pizza pans (or cookie sheets).

If you are making pizza with unbaked homemade (or store-bought) dough, divide the dough into 2 balls and roll each into a 12-inch (30 cm) circle. Place on prepared pizza pans (cookie sheets will do in a pinch) and pinch the edges up slightly.

If you're using one of the alternative crusts below, place in prepared pans.

Either way, spread spaghetti sauce sparingly on each crust (too much sauce makes for a sloppy pizza), sprinkle with cheese, then add whatever toppings you're using. Is that beautiful or what?

Slide your pizzas onto the lowest rack of the oven and bake for 15 minutes, or until the crust is browned and crisp underneath (peek under to check) and the cheese is melted and gooey. Midway through the baking time, you may have to transfer the pans to a higher oven rack to prevent the crust from burning before the topping is done.

Alternative pizza crusts (see below) that are prebaked will be done more quickly because they only need to be baked long enough to melt the cheese and heat the toppings.

Makes two 12-inch (30 cm) pizzas, or however many bigger or smaller ones.

Alternative Pizza Crusts

- store-bought fresh pizza dough (use as if it were your own homemade)
- Italian flatbread shell
- French or Italian bread, cut in half lengthwise
- English muffins
- tortillas
- pita bread

Quesadillas EF

A serious snack that comes dangerously close to being a meal.

> 2 large flour tortillas
> Salsa (mild, medium or hot)
> Shredded Monterey Jack or cheddar cheese
> Other toppings—jalapeños? olives? chocolate chips?
> (just kidding)

Spread a flour tortilla with a generous layer of salsa, almost to the edges. Top with some shredded cheese and whatever other toppings, if any, you might want to add. Then slam another tortilla on top and press the two together.

Place the tortilla "sandwich" in a dry skillet—no butter or oil or anything—over medium heat. Cook, spinning it occasionally to keep it from sticking, until the cheese begins to melt (lift an edge and peek inside). Using a pancake turner, flip the quesadilla and cook the other side for 1 or 2 minutes, until the bottom begins to brown and the cheese inside is completely melted. Slide onto a plate, and cut into wedges like a pizza.

Makes 1 quesadilla. Repeat as needed.

Logical quesadilla deviations

Use spaghetti sauce instead of salsa, mozzarella cheese instead of Monterey Jack and sprinkle in some chopped pepperoni. Voilà! A Pizzadilla.

Add some shredded cooked chicken, pork or beef for something a little more substantial.

Skip the salsa altogether and sprinkle the flour tortilla with crumbled feta cheese and baby spinach leaves. Cook just long enough to melt the cheese and wilt the spinach.

Canned black beans? Leftover chili? Sloppy joe meat? It's all good.

Fully Loaded Nachos GF

Vegetarians can use canned beans or refried beans instead of the meat in these nachos, or just leave out the beans and make Partially Loaded Nachos. Nothing wrong with that.

¾ lb (375 g)	lean ground beef
1	small onion, chopped
1 or 2	fresh jalapeño peppers, chopped
½ cup (125 ml)	salsa (mild or hot—however you like it)
4 cups (1 l)	tortilla chips
2 cups (500 ml)	shredded Monterey Jack or cheddar cheese
	Additional toppings: diced avocado, chopped tomatoes, chopped cilantro, sour cream, more salsa, hot peppers, whatever

Preheat the oven to 400°F (200°C).

Crumble the ground beef into a skillet with the onion and jalapeño peppers, and cook, stirring, over medium heat for 5 to 7 minutes, until the meat is no longer pink. (Or cook the mixture in a microwave on high power for 4 to 6 minutes, stirring once or twice, until the meat is no longer pink.) Remove from heat, drain off any fat and stir in the salsa.

Spread the tortilla chips in a 9 x 13-inch (23 x 33 cm) baking dish. Top with the meat mixture and sprinkle with the cheese. Place in the preheated oven and bake for 10 minutes, or until the cheese is melted.

Top with as many of the additional toppings as you like. Or not. These are good any old way.

This makes enough Fully Loaded Nachos to ruin two people's appetites entirely for dinner.

A Swiss Fondue Evening EF

The snow swirls outside the window of your chalet (your basement apartment) high in the Swiss Alps (down the street from the city dump). A roaring fire blazes in the hearth (the electric heater is on). You gaze romantically (you hope) into the eyes of You-Know-Who as you dunk your bread into the bubbling cheese (and pray you don't drop it down your sleeve). So dreamy.

1 lb (500 g)	Swiss Emmentaler cheese, shredded (about 4 cups/1 l shredded cheese)
3 tbsp (45 ml)	flour
1 clove	garlic, cut in half
2 cups (500 ml)	dry white wine
Dash each	nutmeg and paprika
1 loaf	crusty French or Italian bread, cut into 1-inch (2 cm) cubes

In a large bowl, toss the shredded cheese with the flour to mix.

Rub the inside of your fondue pot or saucepan (see sidebar) with the halved clove of garlic, then discard the garlic. If you are a real garlic fiend, you can chop up the clove and toss it into the pot (but they would never do that in Zurich). Pour the wine into the pot, place it on the stove over medium heat and bring it almost to a boil. Reduce the heat to low.

Add the cheese, 1 handful at a time, to the wine, stirring constantly until cheese is melted. Continue adding handfuls of cheese until it has all mixed into a smooth, creamy sauce. Bring this to a bubble for just a few seconds, then transfer the pot to the fondue burner (if you're using one), or simply lower the heat as much as possible—the sauce should be kept hot, but not allowed to boil. Stir in the nutmeg and paprika.

To serve, spear a cube of bread on the fondue fork (or regular fork), swirl it in the cheese and eat. If you (accidentally) drop your bread into the pot, fondue-eating custom requires you to kiss the person to your right. It's considered bad form, however, to deliberately un-prong another person's bread for sleazy purposes.

Serves 2 to 4 dippers.

How Do You Fondue?

A fondue contraption consists of a medium-size pot that sits in a frame over a small alcohol burner that can go on the table. It comes with a set of long-handled forks. You can find fondue contraptions by the truckload at garage sales and secondhand shops. However, if you don't happen to have an Official Fondue Set, just use a heavy saucepan over low heat on the stove, and regular forks. It won't be quite as romantic, but it'll do the trick.

Focaccia Bread EF

Focaccia is an addictive flatbread—a little like pizza, but without the tomato sauce. If you've never made bread before, this is an easy place to start. Eaten warm from the oven, focaccia makes a fantastic lunch or snack with tomatoes and cheese. Leftovers make an awesome sandwich.

1 recipe	Multipurpose Yeast Dough (recipe on page 163)
2	onions, sliced
¼ cup (50 ml)	olive oil
4 cloves	garlic, minced or pressed
¼ cup (50 ml)	grated Parmesan cheese
1 tsp (5 ml)	dried rosemary or oregano
½ tsp (2 ml)	salt
¼ tsp (1 ml)	black pepper

Grease two cookie sheets or pizza pans.

Heat the oil in a skillet over medium heat. Add the onions and garlic, and cook, stirring occasionally, for 5 to 7 minutes, or until the onions are softened. Let the mixture cool for a couple of minutes.

While the onions are cooling, divide the prepared dough into 2 balls. Working with a blob of dough at a time, flatten it out into an 8-inch (20 cm) circle, about ½ inch (1 cm) thick. Place on the prepared pan and repeat with the second blob. Spread half the onion mixture on each round of dough, leaving some bare dough around the edges. Sprinkle with Parmesan cheese, rosemary or oregano, salt and pepper. Place the breads in a warm place to rise for 20 to 30 minutes until puffy, but not quite doubled in volume.

Preheat your oven to 375°F (190°C).

Place the focaccia in the preheated oven for 20 to 25 minutes, or until the bottom is lightly browned and the top crust is golden.

Everyone will go nuts, so be prepared.

Makes two 10-inch (30 cm) breads.

Mushrooms Masquerading as Escargots GF EF

Escargots (in case you don't already know this) are snails. Regular, ordinary garden snails. Baked in garlic butter, they taste delicious. But so would a pencil eraser. Imagine, then, what that same garlic butter could do for a mushroom. This makes a great appetizer or snack.

½ cup (125 ml)	butter
2 tbsp (30 ml)	finely chopped onion
2 or 3 cloves	garlic, minced or pressed
2 tbsp (30 ml)	finely chopped parsley
½ tsp (2 ml)	salt
¼ tsp (1 ml)	black pepper
24	medium mushrooms, washed and with stalks removed

Preheat the oven to 375°F (190°C).

Melt the butter in a small saucepan over medium heat. Add the chopped onion, garlic and parsley. Stir in the salt and pepper and remove from heat.

Arrange the mushrooms, gill-side up, in a baking dish just big enough to hold them all in a single layer. Spoon the garlic butter over them, making sure the caps are filled. Place in the preheated oven and bake for 15 to 20 minutes, or until the mushrooms are tender. Serve hot with some crusty French bread to soak up the garlicky butter sauce.

Makes 3 or 4 servings.

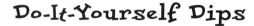

Do-It-Yourself Dips

Why on earth would you go out and buy a ready-made dip when making your own is such a snap? The following dips are divinely delicious and diabolically easy to devour. Definitely.

 ## Dijon Dip EF

½ cup (125 ml)	sour cream (or half sour cream and half plain yogurt)
¼ cup (50 ml)	Dijon mustard
	Salt, pepper, Tabasco sauce

Stir everything together and serve.

 ## Cheese Dip GF EF

2 cups (500 ml)	sour cream
1½ cups (375 ml)	shredded sharp cheddar cheese
¼ cup (50 ml)	pimento-stuffed olives
	Salt and pepper to taste

Throw everything in the blender and whirl.

 ## Dill Pickle Dip GF

1 cup (250 ml)	spreadable cream cheese
½ cup (125 ml)	mayonnaise
¼ cup (50 ml)	finely chopped dill pickle
1 tbsp (15 ml)	finely chopped green onion
1 tsp (5 ml)	pickle juice
	Salt and pepper to taste

Stir everything together and serve.

 ## Curry Dip GF

½ cup (125 ml)	sour cream
½ cup (125 ml)	mayonnaise
2 tsp (10 ml)	curry powder
1 clove	garlic, squished
	Salt and pepper to taste

Stir it all together and dip.

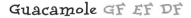

Guacamole GF EF DF

The best thing to happen to a tortilla chip—ever. Also *muy bueno* on a taco or burrito, and *magnifico* on your nachos.

2	large, fully ripe avocados
1	small red onion, finely chopped
1	medium tomato, finely chopped
1	fresh jalapeño pepper, seeded and finely chopped
¼ cup (50 ml)	chopped fresh cilantro
2 tbsp (30 ml)	fresh lime juice
½ tsp (2 ml)	salt

Cut the avocados in half, remove the pits and peel the avocados. If they're ripe, the peel will come off easily. Dice the avocado flesh and place it in a bowl. Add the onion, tomato, jalapeño, cilantro, lime juice and salt. Mash gently—don't puree this; it should stay chunky. Taste, and adjust the seasoning with a little more of this or that if you want.

Makes about 1½ cups (375 ml) guacamole.

Pita Crisps

Give your pita bread a second life! Reincarnate that stale package of pita as a crunchy snack. Easy, delicious and everyone will think you're a recycling genius.

Preheat the oven to 200°F (100°C).

Carefully split each pita bread into 2 separate layers and arrange these on a large baking sheet, inside-surface up. It really doesn't matter if you rip the breads. You'll be breaking them up afterward anyway.

Pour a little olive oil, vegetable oil or melted butter into a small dish. Stir in a squished clove of garlic (two, if you're feeling wild). Using a pastry brush (or a clean paintbrush), brush the rough surface of the pita breads with the garlic–oil mixture. Sprinkle with salt, pepper and whatever other seasonings you like (oregano, cayenne, parsley and so on). Bake in the preheated oven until crisp and golden—45 minutes to 1 hour. Check occasionally as they bake to make sure they're not burning.

Break up the pita into smaller pieces, and serve with dip, salad, soup or all by itself as a snack.

Hummus GF EF DF

**Better than store-bought, homemade hummus takes no time to
make. Go ahead—give it a whirl.**

1 can (19 oz/540 ml)	chickpeas, drained (but save the liquid)
¼ cup (50 ml)	tahini (sesame paste—available in most supermarkets or in Middle Eastern and health food stores)
¼ cup (50 ml)	lemon juice
2 cloves	garlic
½ tsp (2 ml)	ground cumin (optional)
½ tsp (2 ml)	salt

In the container of a blender or food processor, combine the chickpeas,
¼ cup (50 ml) of the chickpea liquid, tahini, lemon juice, garlic,
cumin and salt. Blend until really smooth, scraping down the sides 2
or 3 times with a scraper. Hummus should be a little thicker than, say,
sour cream. If it's too thick, add a little more of the reserved chickpea
liquid. Taste, and adjust the seasoning if necessary. Scoop into a bowl,
sprinkle the top with a little chopped parsley and serve with pita bread
or vegetable dippers.

Makes about 2 cups of hummus.

Hummus gone wild!

Stuck in a hummus rut? Tired of the same old same old? Time for
a change! Here are some variations to kick your hummus out of the
doldrums.

- Roasted Red Pepper Hummus: add one jarred roasted red pepper to
  the blender.
- Hot and Spicy Hummus: toss in a healthy dash of cayenne pepper
  and a fresh jalapeño.
- Tomato and Basil Hummus: add ¼ cup (50 ml) oil-packed sun-
  dried tomatoes and 1 tbsp (15 ml) fresh basil leaves.
- Olive Hummus: add ¼ cup (50 ml) pitted red, black or pimento-
  stuffed olives.

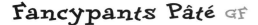

Fancypants Pâté GF

Liver gets no respect. But call it pâté, serve it with some fancy crackers—and *oo la la! C'est formidable!*

2 tbsp (30 ml)	olive oil or vegetable oil
1 or 2 cloves	garlic, squished
1 lb (500 g)	chicken livers, cut into halves
1 tbsp (15 ml)	finely chopped fresh parsley
½ cup (125 ml)	softened butter
½ tsp (2 ml)	salt
¼ tsp (1 ml)	black pepper

Heat the oil in a skillet over medium-low heat. Add the garlic and cook gently until softened—about 2 minutes. Add the chicken livers, raise the heat to medium high and cook, stirring them in the pan, until browned on the outside but still a little pink inside when you cut them open—about 5 minutes. Add the parsley, cook for another minute and remove from heat.

Scoop the livers (and all the liquid in the pan) into the container of a blender or food processor. Add the softened butter, salt and pepper. Zip this around, scraping the sides down occasionally, until the mixture is completely pureed and smooth.

Pack the pâté into a small dish or crock, cover it with plastic wrap and refrigerate at least 4 hours or overnight, so that it firms up. Serve with crackers or French bread. And your very best French accent.

Makes about 2 cups (500 ml) of pâté.

How to Make a Good Cup of Coffee

There are several good ways to make a cup of coffee, and each method has its rabid fans. Here are three of the most common ways to get your daily dose of caffeine. Pick the one that suits your style. As for the coffee itself, the choices are endless. Buy the best coffee you can afford and keep it fresh in a tightly closed container, preferably refrigerated.

Electric Drip Coffee

You'll need an electric drip coffeemaker for this. Easy enough to find, even secondhand. You'll also need paper filters that fit your machine.

Place a paper filter in the basket of your machine. Measure about 1 tbsp (15 ml) finely ground coffee for each cup of coffee you will be making. Add an extra spoonful for good luck. Fill water reservoir with fresh cold water. Flip the switch and you're done. Nothing to it.

Manual Drip Coffee

You'll need a cone-shaped filter holder and something, like a glass or thermal carafe, for the coffee to drip into. If you get a small single-cup filter holder, you can drip the coffee directly into your mug. Cheap, easy and portable.

Place the correct-size paper filter in the filter holder and set it over the carafe or mug. Add 1 tbsp (15 ml) finely ground coffee for each cup of coffee you're making, plus a bit extra (a whole extra spoonful for a full pot, less for a single mug). Boil fresh water in a kettle. Pour just enough water into the coffee filter to wet the grounds, let sit for 30 seconds, then pour the remaining water over the grounds gradually and allow the water to drip through. Done.

French Press

The only equipment you'll need is a French press coffeepot. This is a glass cylinder with a sort of plunger-filter contraption built into the lid. These often show up at secondhand stores and garage sales.

Boil some water in a kettle. Remove the plunger gizmo from the press pot. For each 8 oz (250 ml) of water you'll be pouring into the pot, measure 2 tbsp (30 ml) of coarse or regular ground coffee into the bottom of the cylinder. Pour in the boiling water, stir and gently place the lid contraption on top—don't press yet. Let the coffee steep for 4 minutes. After 4 minutes, slowly press on the plunger until it reaches the bottom. The coffee grounds are trapped beneath the filter plunger. Put on your French beret and write a poem while you enjoy *un bon café*.

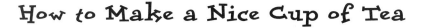

How to Make a Nice Cup of Tea

What Kind?

Regular everyday black tea is made from the fermented leaves of the tea bush. Black tea contains caffeine (like coffee) and is what most people think of as tea. It's available in tea bags or loose. You can find all kinds—some with fruit or flavors added, others processed in particular ways. Black tea may be called Orange Pekoe or Earl Grey or Darjeeling or English Breakfast or some other such thing. Try several varieties and discover which you like best.

Green tea is made from leaves that have not been fermented so the tea retains the green color of the leaves. Green tea is available in tea bags and loose. There are also many different kinds of green tea, each with its own flavor and characteristics.

Herbal teas are made from various herbs, fruits and spices. These are generally caffeine-free, and tend to have funky names like Midnight Mango and Nutmeg Nirvana. You're on your own here—there are a lot to choose from.

Method

Fill your kettle or saucepan with fresh, cold water. Bring it to a full boil. Meanwhile, rinse your cup or teapot out with hot water and put in your tea bag or bags (assuming you're using tea bags, not loose tea).

Use 1 tea bag for every 2 cups of boiling water. So, for example, if your teapot holds 4 cups of water, use 2 tea bags. Pour in the boiling water and let the tea steep for 5 minutes. Remove the tea bag(s) before serving.

If you're using loose tea, use 1 tsp (5 ml) per cup of water. The method is the same as for tea bags, but you'll have to strain out the leaves or pour carefully so that they remain in the teapot.

Regular tea is usually served with milk and sugar. Some people prefer it with honey and lemon (no milk), and others like it just plain, with nothing. Suit yourself. Herbal tea should be served with honey or sugar—*never* with milk. And green tea is most often taken straight—no milk, no sugar, no nothing.

How to Plan a Meal

The Beginning

This is the part of the meal that gets everyone interested and gives the cook time to (madly) finish making the rest of dinner. You might just serve some veggies and dip. Or a bag of pretzels. Or even beluga caviar on toasts (but not bloody likely). Don't go overboard on the starters unless you expect the main course to be inedible or terribly late—and try to avoid serving a food that will appear again later in the meal.

The Middle

Here we have your basic meat and potatoes section, where you will generally find your main dish. Of course, it doesn't have to be meat and potatoes. It can be lasagna and salad, beans and rice, or tuna casserole and broccoli. There's nothing really *wrong* with the usual formula of one meat thing, one starch thing and one vegetable thing, except that it's not the only way to plan a meal. Try to vary tastes and textures, but don't attempt to make too many different dishes, because you'll drive yourself crazy. Sometimes one great dish with a loaf of good bread is more than enough.

Artistically speaking, avoid monochromatic meals. A dinner of white chicken, white potatoes and white cauliflower might taste just fine, but it looks really depressing on a plate. An all-black dinner is even worse. And unless it's Saint Patrick's Day, a totally green meal would be just plain weird. Go multicolor.

The Ending

Ah, dessert. The happy ending to a wonderful meal. Or maybe the happy ending to a not-so-great meal. Whatever the story, it's definitely what everyone has been waiting for. Will it be your famous Hot Fudge Pudding? Will it be spectacular Bananas Flambé? Or will it be (drat) sensible, nutritious fruit? Most of the time you should probably go the sensibly nutritious route. But once in a while something gooey and decadent is very therapeutic. Aim for a balance.

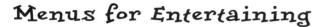

Menus for Entertaining

The artsy vegetarian girl/boyfriend

Antipasto—arranged very artistically, including at least a couple of really quirky items
Pasta with perfect pesto
Sliced tomatoes with basil and olive oil
Very good Italian bread
Fresh fruit—the more exotic the better

The intellectual girl/boyfriend

Pita crisps with hummus
Mostly Moroccan vegetable couscous
Tomato, cucumber and feta salad with Zorba the Greek dressing
Crème caramel

Conservative but intriguing girl/boyfriend

Mushrooms masquerading as escargots
Curry glazed chicken
Brown rice
Steamed fresh asparagus
Crunchy cucumber salad
Pineapple upside-down cake

Shallow but fun girl/boyfriend

Veggies and mustard dip
Spaghetti with meatballs
Tomato and basil bruschetta
Green salad with desperation ranch dressing
Antidepressant brownies with ice cream

Desperately, madly, (almost stupidly) in love

Fancypants pâté with crackers
Swiss fondue
An extremely interesting green salad with vinaigrette dressing
Bananas flambé

The thrill is gone dinner

Tortilla chips with salsa
Potato paprikash with hot dogs
Coleslaw with creamy dressing
Official peanut butter cookies

Mom and Dad for dinner (with optional younger siblings)

Veggies with cheese dip
X-ray vision soup
Incredible garlic chicken with crusty whole grain bread
Steamed broccoli
White or brown rice
Romaine lettuce salad with vinaigrette dressing
Carrot cake with cream cheese icing

Your best friend is depressed

Minestrone soup
Focaccia bread
A big salad with slightly caesar dressing
Self-saucing hot fudge pudding with ice cream

Your sweetie has a cold (awwwww)

Chicken soup with noodles
Irish soda bread (warm from the oven, of course)
Earl Grey tea
Rainy day rice pudding

Buncha galoots for dinner

Veggies with dips (plenty of everything)
Lasagna to die for
High-voltage garlic bread
Mixed green salad with creamy Italian dressing
Chocolate cake with chocolate icing

Happy birthday to yoooou!

Guacamole with tortilla chips
Hawaiian meatballs
White rice
Mixed green salad with Zorba the Greek dressing
Almond torte with mocha cream icing

Video watch-a-thon evening (also suitable for big sports things on TV)

Fully loaded nachos
Thermonuclear buffalo wings
Veggie sticks with mustard dip
Homemade pizza
Idiotproof yellow cake with chocolate icing

Slightly sophisticated brunch

Gazpacho
Cheese and bread strata
Mixed green salad with vinaigrette dressing, sprinkled with slivered almonds and dried cranberries
Banana bread, cinnamon swirl coffee cake

Aunt Gladys for lunch

Potato soup
Unfettered frittata with crusty Italian or French bread
Absolutely normal lettuce salad with creamy Italian dressing
Fresh fruit plate—regular things like oranges, grapes, peaches, apples

Cooking Terminology Demystified

Mince, sauté, deglaze—what exactly are they asking us to do and is it decent?

Bake To cook in an oven. You know—like a cake.

Baste Like when you use sunscreen at the beach. You baste foods like turkey to keep them moist while they're roasting.

Beat To clobber the daylights out of, let's say, an egg. Can be done by hand with a whisk or fork, or in an electric mixer.

Blend To combine ingredients into a uniform mixture.

Boil Scientifically speaking, to bring a liquid to 212°F (100°C) until it gets hot and bubbly.

Braise To cook for a long time over low heat with a little liquid in a covered pan.

Bread To coat a food—like chicken or fish—in bread crumbs before frying.

Broil Under the broiler element of an oven— sort of like an upside-down barbecue.

Chop To cut up into little pieces. Bigger than minced, but smaller than diced.

Cream To mush together soft ingredients—like butter and sugar—to make a creamy mixture.

Curdle A disgusting effect that happens to certain sauces or liquids when they are overcooked—yucky, lumpy, separated clumps.

Dash Oh, just a squirt or two.

Deglaze You deglaze a pan by pouring a little liquid into it, then cooking to dissolve the brown bits stuck on the bottom. Makes a nice gravy and cuts down on dishwashing.

Dice Bigger than chopped (see above). Usually in little square-ish shapes.

Dredge To lightly coat a food with flour or crumbs. Who would have guessed?

Drizzle What happens when you forget your umbrella. Just kidding. Actually, to pour a thin stream of liquid over food.

Drop What a person asks for when they really want more. As in, "I'll just have another tiny *drop* of lasagna."

Dunk What you do to your chocolate chip cookie in a glass of milk.

Fold To very gently mix one ingredient into another using a spatula to lift from underneath. Don't try to do this when you're in a big hurry.

Fry The f-word. To cook food in a pan with plenty of oil, resulting in either delicious crispness or greasy sog. Depending.

Garnish That little sprig of parsley beside the mashed potatoes. The slice of orange next to the chicken. The paprika on the potato salad. Most commonly found in restaurants where they have time to do this sort of thing.

Grate To put through the holes of a grater, usually resulting in shreddy little pieces. Cheese is the most common victim of this process. Also knuckles. Be careful.

Grease To coat a pan with, yes, *grease* (butter, vegetable oil or shortening, nonstick cooking spray) so that food doesn't stick.

Julienne Thin strands of any kind of food that doesn't naturally occur in that shape—such as long strings of carrot, zucchini or ham.

Knead To mangle a lump of dough by hand in order to make it smooth and uniform. Usually associated with bread dough. Excellent for venting frustration.

Leavening Any substance that is used to cause a mixture to rise while baking—like yeast or baking powder.

Marinate To soak food in a liquid in order to tenderize it or add flavor.

Mash To squash with a fork or masher. Made famous by potatoes.

Melt To turn a solid into a liquid. Sometimes, unfortunately, it happens by accident to your ice cream cone.

Meringue The best part of a lemon pie. A fluffy substance made of stiffly beaten egg whites and sugar.

Mince Smaller than either diced or chopped (see page 209). Little eensy bits.

Mix Just stir it together, with a spoon or fork or your hands or a shovel. Depending.

Peel To remove the outside of a fruit or vegetable—the part that your mother told you has all the vitamins.

Pinch YOW! Don't *do* that! Just a tiny bit more than a dash (see page 209).

Pit To remove the seed, usually of a fruit.

Poach To cook in gently simmering (see below) water.

Pound What you'd like to do to that idiot who wrecked your bike. In food, to flatten.

Preheat To turn your oven on ahead of time, so that it will be at the right temperature when you put the cake in.

Puree To mash or blend a solid food into a smooth, lump-free mixture.

Roast Really, this is the same as bake (see page 209), except that it's generally associated with meat. You wouldn't, for example, *roast* a cake.

Sauté But of course, zees ees to cook zee food in zee pan weeth just a *petit* leetle bit of zee oil or zee butter. *Oo la la.*

Scorch What happens when you go answer the phone while your spaghetti sauce is boiling, resulting in a black residue on the bottom of the pot, a nasty burned taste and smell and a lot of bad words. Avoid, avoid, avoid!

Scramble What you do to an egg with a fork.

Shred To cut or grate something into long thin pieces.

Sift What you do to flour in order to remove any lumps and to fluff it up.

Simmer Almost boiling, *but not quite.* Little tiny bubbles.

Sliver A thin strip. *Except* when used in the sentence "I'll have just a *sliver* of pumpkin pie," where it actually means a huge slab.

Steam To cook food in a basket or strainer suspended over (but not touching) boiling water. Especially useful for vegetables.

Stew To cook something for a long time in a covered pan with liquid.

Stir To mix with a spoon.

Stir-fry Tossing and stirring cut-up bits of food in a very hot pan with oil. Very fast, very dramatic. Also very messy if you're not careful.

Stock Broth, basically. Can be made with meat or vegetables or fish.

Strain To remove the solid bits from a liquid. You know—like when you have those floaty little things you hate in your orange juice.

Toss Mixing enthusiastically! Yahoo!

Whip Like beat (see above) but even *more* so. You do this to cream and egg whites.

Whisk To beat with a (*surprise*) whisk. What you do to a sauce, for instance, to get the lumps out.

Zest The colored outside peel of an orange or lemon. Also the act of removing that part.

The Clueless Guide to Metric Conversion

Unless you happen to be a nuclear physicist, it's not necessary to convert cooking measurements with extreme precision. Close is usually good enough. The following table will give you the metric equivalent for both imperial and U.S. measurements.

Metric Conversion Weight

U.S. unit	Imperial unit	Metric equivalent
1 pound 16 ounces	1 pound 16 ounces	500 grams
2 pounds	2 pounds	1 kilogram
½ pound 8 ounces	½ pound 8 ounces	250 grams
¼ pound 4 ounces	¼ pound 4 ounces	125 grams

Metric Conversion Volume

U.S. unit	Imperial unit	Metric equivalent
1 U.S. gallon 128 fluid ounces 4 U.S. quarts	1 imperial gallon 160 fluid ounces 4 imperial quarts	4 liters
1 U.S. quart 32 fluid ounces 4 cups	1 imperial quart 40 fluid ounces 5 cups	1 liter
1 U.S. pint 16 fluid ounces 2 cups	1 imperial pint 20 fluid ounces 2½ cups	½ liter 500 milliliters
1 cup 8 fluid ounces 16 tablespoons	1 cup 8 fluid ounces 16 tablespoons	250 milliliters
½ cup 4 fluid ounces 8 tablespoons	½ cup 4 fluid ounces 8 tablespoons	125 milliliters

Metric Conversion Volume

¼ cup	¼ cup	75 milliliters
¼ cup 2 fluid ounces 4 tablespoons	¼ cup 2 fluid ounces 4 tablespoons	50 milliliters
1 tablespoon 3 teaspoons	1 tablespoon 3 teaspoons	15 milliliters
1 teaspoon	1 teaspoon	5 milliliters
½ teaspoon	½ teaspoon	2 milliliters
¼ teaspoon	¼ teaspoon	1 milliliters

Metric Conversion Temperature

U.S. Imperial unit	Metric equivalent
200° Fahrenheit	100° Celsius
250° Fahrenheit	120° Celsius
275° Fahrenheit	140° Celsius
300° Fahrenheit	150° Celsius
325° Fahrenheit	160° Celsius
350° Fahrenheit	180° Celsius
375° Fahrenheit	190° Celsius
400° Fahrenheit	200° Celsius
425° Fahrenheit	220° Celsius
450° Fahrenheit	230° Celsius

Metric Conversion Pan Sizes

U.S. Imperial unit	Metric equivalent
8-inch pan	20-centimeter pan
9-inch pan	23-centimeter pan
10-inch pan	25-centimeter pan
9 x 13-inch pan	23 x 33-centimeter pan
10 x 15-inch pan	35 x 40-centimeter pan

Index

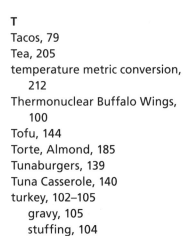